With Michael Collins In The Fight For Irish Independence

by

Batt O'Connor, TD

Ann,
I really enjoyed
having you to stay,
especially in Glandore,
I hope you enjoyed it as

Cover Design:
Timothy Lane

much as I did!
I Hope it won't be Too
long again before we meet
where ever!! love Cal.

Aubane Historical Society
Aubane
Millstreet
Co. Cork

Books From The Aubane Historical Society:

* **Ned Buckley's Poems**
* **A North Cork Anthology**, by Jack Lane and B. Clifford
* **Local Evidence to the Devon Commission**, by Jack Lane
* **Spotlights On Irish History**, by Brendan Clifford: Battles of Knocknanoss & Knockbrack, Edmund Burke, The Famine, The Civil War, John Philpot Curran, Daniel O'Connell and Roy Foster's approach to history.
* **The 'Cork Free Press' In The Context Of The Parnell Split**: The Restructuring Of Ireland, 1890-1910, by Brendan Clifford
* **Aubane: Where In The World Is It?** A Microcosm Of Irish History In A Cork Townland, by Jack Lane
* **Piarais Feiritéir: Dánta/Poems**, with Translations by Pat Muldowney
  Audio tape of a selection of the poems by Bosco O'Conchuir
* **Elizabeth Bowen: "Notes On Eire".** Espionage Reports to Winston Churchill, 1940-42; With a Review of Irish Neutrality in WW II by Jack Lane and Brendan Clifford
* **Thomas Davis**, by Charles Gavan Duffy
* **Selections from 'The Nation'**, 1842-44.
* **Na hAislingí—vision poems of Eoghan Ruadh O'Súilleabháin** translated by Pat Muldowney, with Revisionist History of the 18th century under the Spotlight, by Brendan Clifford
* **Sean Moylan. In His Own Words.**

With Michael Collins In The Fight For Irish Independence
by
Batt O'Connor
2004
ISBN 1 903497 17 5

Aubane Historical Society
www.atholbooks.org/ahs/index.shtml

Secretary: Noreen Kelleher, Telephone 029 70 360

Orders: jacklaneaubane@hotmail.com

Contents

Sean Moylan. In His Own Words.

His Memoir of the War of Independence,

with a selection of his speeches and poems.

Preface: *Jack Lane,*

Introduction: *Éamon Ó Cuív,*

Epilogue: *Brendan Clifford.*

Available from:
The Aubane Historical Society
www.atholbooks.org/ahs/index.shtml

Introduction

Bartholomew O'Connor (1870-1935) was a stonemason from Brosna, Co. Kerry, who became a bricklayer and a Republican in Boston. On returning to Ireland he became a successful builder in Dublin (where Sean Moylan worked for him as a carpenter), and also a member of the Gaelic League and the Irish Republican Brotherhood. He was not engaged in the fighting in 1916 but was interned along with those who were. It was in his capacity as a successful builder that he became closely associated with Michael Collins in the Anglo-Irish War of 1919-21, providing him with hiding places around Dublin. He supported Collins over the Treaty, but doesn't seem to have played an active military part in the Treaty War. He was elected to the Free State Dail for Co. Dublin in 1924 as a member of *Cumann na nGaedheal*, formed from the Treatyite wing of Sinn Fein. His book was published by Peter Davies, London, in 1929. It is not just another book about Michael Collins. The first half of it, which is not the least interesting part, is about O'Connor himself. It is unpretentious, easily readable, matter-of-fact and transparently honest—and it must appear painfully naive and fundamentalist to the sophisticated mind of the present-day revisionist, even though revisionist history bases itself on the Treaty and O'Connor was an unrepentant Treatyite to the end.

I find that Batt O'Connor has been largely forgotten. He is not even a name to many people who are well-informed about the War of Independence. Dan Breen's Book is generally known about, as are Tom Barry's Book, and Ernie O'Malley's Book, even by people who have not read them. But Batt O'Connor's book did not become Batt O'Connor's Book. The reason might be that he is the odd man out in that group. He is the Treatyite who wrote a book of Republican memoirs—and the Treaty failed. At least it failed to sustain the Republican momentum, even though Collins had billed it as a stepping-stone to the Republic.

Batt O'Connor was still remembered in the 1950s in the part of *Slieve Luacra* where I grew up, and I have always had a pretty accurate idea of what he was. It might be that I read his book, though I don't recall it. But I grew up amongst people who remembered him, and therefore I knew how he was known—it was with a blend of admiration and regret. (Brosna is on the Kerry fringe of the Cork/ Kerry/ Limerick borderland, which constitutes a highly distinctive cultural region. I suppose there was a particular memory of O'Connor in North-West Cork because he was taken to be a local man.

But there are considerable differences within that general locality, as I tried to explain in my book on James Clarence Mangan. I was accustomed to hearing everything under the sun discussed as I grew up. Many of the battles of the War of Independence had been fought there, and that was possibly why it got through the Treaty War with no great damage to itself, and people settled down to the new party-politics very quickly, and everything was discussed. But, on the Kerry side, where there was less action in the War of Independence, things were done in the Treaty War which did not bear speaking about.)

I have looked up the Obituaries on O'Connor in the four daily newspapers and found little in them that was not in his book. the most interesting things were a comment in the *Irish Press*, and the long list of people of all political tendencies attending his funeral.

There were many leading anti-Treatyites among O'Connor's mourners. Sean Moylan, Sean MacEntee and Dan Breen were at the Removal of Remains and De Valera and Sean T. O'Kelly attended the funeral.

(The *Irish Press*, which irresponsibly ceased publication some years ago with an unbalancing effect on Irish public life, was the anti-Treaty paper— the paper of the *Fianna Fail* party, which came to power three years before O'Connor's death and resumed the Republican development of the state. Its Editor was Frank Gallagher whose career in political journalism began on the *Cork Free Press*, the daily paper of the All-For-Ireland League which defeated the Redmondite Home Rulers in all but one of the Co. Cork constituencies in the 1910 Elections. The AFIL attacked the Redmondites for bringing Catholic-sectarianism to dominance in Home Rule politics, and put forward *"Conciliation"* as the watchword of its alternative approach. With such a source it is not surprising that the *Irish Press* was the most liberal and tolerant, as well as the most hard-headed, of the Irish papers.)

In its obituary notice on 7th February, the *Irish Press* commented:

> "During the Anglo-Irish struggle he was an active helper of Collins. It was to be expected, therefore, that with the signing of the 'Treaty', he would follow the course adopted by his associate in supporting the settlement."

The effective meaning is that he was carried along by his special relationship with Collins and this was not to be held against him—an attitude which, though perhaps patronising, was not unfriendly.

It did not mean that in the view of the *Irish Press* the 'Treaty' had ceased to be a matter of immediate consequence. The dispute with Britain over the terms imposed by the Treaty, which began in 1932, ran on until about 1940.

One flare-up in the dispute coincided with O'Connor's funeral. The British Colonial Secretary made a speech condemning the latest breach by Dublin of the terms of the treaty. He said in the course of it:

"The only quarrel we have with the Free State is a quarrel over what is called the sanctity of agreements. Fundamentally the sanctity of agreements is something that must be maintained at all costs".

The *Irish Press* commented:

"Mr. Thomas showed an unexpected wisdom in his qualifying phrase 'what is called'. The agreement to which he particularly refers... is the 'Treaty', a document to which the British signatories themselves have confessed was signed by Irishmen only under the threat of savage war upon the Irish people. There was no sanctity about the signing of that 'agreement', there was no sanctity about it when the Dail majority approved it as the alternative to war, and there is no sanctity about it now. 'Brought about by force, it lasts only so long as force can maintain it', says Mr. de Valera in his comment on Mr. Thomas' speech" (15 February, 1935).

(The Colonial Secretary was former Trade Union leader, J.H. Thomas, who was in the early 1930s a Labour representative in the all-party Coalition by which Britain was governed from 1931 to 1945.)

O'Connor's outlook is that of the Fenian Brotherhood, the IRB—the outlook of the revolutionary elite of the national movement which operated conspiratorially and sought opportunities to involve the populace in conflict with the Imperial state. Given a free choice the populace would have chosen independence. But there was no freedom of choice. Independence was not available. What was available was subordination to the British state with or without a modest degree of devolved government. The electorate—which in the last Election before 1918 was still only about a third of the adult population despite a series of franchise reforms since 1832—voted for subordinate local government, which was called Home Rule. A decision for independence would have been a decision for war, and the disparity between the maximum force that nationalist Ireland could muster and the amount of force routinely available to the British state in Ireland was so great, that an Irish victory in an Anglo-Irish War appeared to be a total impossibility.

There was no abhorrence of political violence as such in Irish society. It had for more than a century contributed a major part of the bulk of the British Army during a period when Britain was continuously engaged in aggressive acts of political violence around the world. But it had lost the habit of engaging in political violence on its own behalf. That habit had been suppressed in the long draconian pacification that followed the Williamite conquest of the 1690s. The country became a reserve of military manpower for the British Empire about three generations after its own will had been broken by *"Derry, Aughrim, Enniskillen and the Boyne"*. It came to abhor all political violence except that into which it was commanded by the masterful English state, and it even lost the sense that what it did in the service of the English state was political violence. And yet it did not become an integral part of the political life of this state whose military needs it served. It retained a sense of distinct nationality but, in the development of its national interest, it was disabled by the ingrained pacifism of its relationship with the English state—a pacifism which was only compounded by the military service which it unquestioningly rendered to the English state.

There had been direct action against landlord oppression at various moments during the 19th century, but they were local in character, and the state could deal with them as mere acts of disorder even while enacting some reforms in response to them. There was an attempt at rebellion in 1848, but it was a mere act of desperation provoked by desperate circumstances. In 1867 the attempted rebellion of the Fenian conspiracy was seen off by the greater conspiratorial power of the state. In 1882 the tighter conspiracy of the Invincibles achieved a spectacular assassination. A quarter of a century of extensive social reform driven by purposeful agitation followed. And then that quarter century of effective constitutional action ended in the first Irish military action against the British state since the time of Sarsfield—the first Irish act of political violence to which the term *military* can be properly applied. (In 1798 the Wexford rebellion was a provoked act of desperation; in Antrim and Down there was an elaborately prepared military takeover from which those who had made the preparations pulled out at the eleventh hour; and the sustained military action in Connaught was French.)

The attempted rebellion of 1848 was an act of desperation provoked by utilitarian British manipulation of the Famine. It failed utterly, as acts of desperation often do. 1916 was a deliberately arranged act of provocation on the Irish side. The Irish on this occasion acted as deliberately as the British state generally does when it engages in acts of war. The Rising was not a reflex action in circumstances of desperation. It was an independent act of statecraft. It enlisted the tradition of two hundred years in its Proclamation but it was itself different in kind from anything that was done in those two hundred years. It was crushed after a spectacular battle lasting almost a week. But, because its appeal was not to the desperation of the country but to its sense of freedom, it had immediate consequences, both political and military. The old arts of Imperial government did not work in a country that was experiencing an unprecedented degree of affluence after two centuries of misery, and that had for two years been fighting as an active component of the British Empire in the Great War which it had been told was a war for Democracy and the Freedom of small nations. The reforms enacted for the purpose of *"killing Home Rule with kindness"*, did, in the end, kill Home Rule alright by allowing the growth of a generalised sense of freedom,and the sentiments appealed to in the recruiting propaganda of the Great War against the Hun began to be applied at home. (These developments are amply and readably described in Dr. Pat Walsh's book, *The Rise And Fall Of Imperial Ireland*, Athol Books 2003, dealing with events in Ireland and Britain between the Boer War and the Easter Rising.)

Batt O'Connor tells how the IRB, directed by Michael Collins, supervised the national resurgence that followed the suppression of the Rising. In fact the most influential person in Ireland in the critical period immediately following the Rising was Mrs. Tom Clarke. The strings of the Fenian conspiracy were handed over to Kathleen Clarke by her husband. She provided the continuity of organised action which harnessed the spontaneous response to the Rising, and later on she selected Michael Collins for the part he was to play. (See Kathleen Clarke's Memoirs.)

O'Connor tells of his disagreement with Cathal Brugha over the continuing activity of the IRB. Brugha, like De Valera, was by nature a democrat rather than a conspirator. They recognised that conspiracy was necessary under the authoritarian British regime, but thought it had served its purpose when it brought about the Rising.

I think it is doubtful that the democracy would have developed as strongly and coherently as it did in 1917-18 without the continuous activity behind the scenes of the conspiracy. In complex, difficult and dangerous situations, sustained and purposeful activity of the mass of society is usually the sign that some kind of conspiracy is at work. If Kathleen Clarke had dispersed the IRB in 1916, that would have left the British state with a purely spontaneous flux to manipulate—and the British state in Ireland has always been a highly organised conspiracy: as indeed it has in great part been in Britain itself, where the organised party structures of the ruling class long preceded the process of gradual democratisation that began in 1832 and shaped the democracy into pre-existing moulds. The IRB is in that regard best understood, in 1916-1918, as being equivalent to the Whig oligarchy around 1830. But its very success brought about a general democratic development that was beyond its control. And that is something that rankled with Batt O'Connor in connection with the Treaty. In 1916, "Nearly all the people of the village were hostile". In 1919 a solid citizen in Dublin thought it wiser not to become personally acquainted with Collins, but:

"That timid gentleman was afterwards an opponent of the Treaty. I met

him early in 1922 in the Munster and Leinster Bank. Expanding his chest and assuming a heroic posture, he told me that nothing less than a Republic would satisfy him. *'Right you are!'* said I. *'But before setting up a Republic we'll have to beat the English out of Ireland. The day is not long past when I saw you slinking out of my house'*, I cried, seizing him by the lapel of his coat, *'because Michael Collins was under the same roof with you'*."
The awkward thing about democracy is that it is democratic!

What O'Connor says in this paragraph conflicts with what he says in the chapter on the Treaty: "The Treaty was made with the Irish people as the people of a belligerent nation"; and it "secured the recognition of Dail Eireann as the *de jure* Parliament in Dublin".

Dail Eireann had made a declaration of Irish independence as a Republic. That was the *de jure* position. It repudiated British jurisdiction and therefore did not look to the Imperial power to confer *de jure* validity on it. America traces its independence *de jure* to its own proclamation of it in 1776 even though a corresponding *de facto* position took some time to achieve. It does not commemorate the *Treaty of Paris* of 1783, in which Britain eventually acknowledged American independence, as the event which gave it birth.

The 1916 Proclamation set in motion the series of events which led to the democratic triumph of Republicanism in 1918 and the Declaration of Independence in January 1919. The Election confirmed what the IRB had proclaimed. Either date might be taken as marking the birth of Irish independence *de jure*. If the electoral mandate is considered essential, then the date is January 1919. Present-day revisionist historians (shepherded by Oxford University) take the Treaty as the event that established Irish independence *de jure*, as O'Connor does. But then O'Connor goes on to say, after the signing of the Treaty, that the maintenance of what the Dail had declared would require another war with Britain. This is an admission that the Treaty was an accommodation with the Imperial power made under duress.

The Treaty quite specifically did *not* recognise the Dail. The members of the Dail who accepted the Treaty had to meet as the Parliament of Southern Ireland under the 1920 *Government of Ireland Act* in order to avail of its terms.

The 1935 *Irish Press* comment quoted above puts the word 'Treaty' in quotation marks, because it was not a Treaty at all, but an Agreement made between the sovereign power and the elite of the rebellion. Treaties are made between sovereign powers. Britain did not recognise the Dail as the Parliament of a sovereign power nor did it confer sovereignty on it under the *"Treaty"*.

Independence was asserted *de jure* by the Dail in January 1919. It was not fully established *de facto*, in the face of vastly superior British military force, by 1921. Britain made an Agreement with a section of the Republican movement—the elite section—in 1921, and armed it to suppress the other section in 1922. The setting up of the Free State involved a submission *de jure* to Imperial authority in exchange for the recognition by Britain of a substantial degree of internal *de facto* authority within the 26 Counties by the institutions set up under its aegis.

De jure independence was democratically asserted in 1919, and re-asserted in 1937 when a new Constitution was freely adopted in place of the dictated Constitution of 1922. *De facto* independence can be taken as being fully achieved in 1940 when De Valera's Government faced down Churchill's threats.

Churchill claimed that, by the terms of the 1921 Agreement (the *"Treaty"*), the Irish Government had no right to be at peace with the King's enemies when the King was at war with them. The rights of the Crown lapsed in Ireland when the Minister of the Crown failed to enforce them in a situation in which the Crown had need of them. But those rights were not given up by the Crown when it signed the *"Treaty"*. (As far as I know they have never been formally revoked.)

The reason things worked out as they did in Ireland after 1922 was not that a British recognition of Irish independence was somehow implicit in the 'Treaty'. The reason was that Britain suffered a considerable collapse of Imperial will in the Autumn of 1922,when the Turkish defiance led to the fall of the Lloyd George Coalition and ushered in a generation of weak Governments composed of what Churchill contemptuously described as *"second elevens"*, and that the anti-Treaty party came to power in 1932.

In the early 1930s Britain made a Treaty with a subordinate Government which it had established in Iraq which was very similar to its Irish Agreement of 1921-2. Iraq, like Ireland, declared neutrality when Britain launched its Second World War in 1939. When Churchill wanted to invade Iran in 1941 using Iraq as a base, he judged that the Iraqi Government was not being sufficiently compliant under the terms of the Treaty, declared it to be in revolt, overthrew it by force, and installed a puppet Government. The chief reason he did not act similarly in Ireland was his desperate need to draw the United States into his War as an ally, and the influence of Irish-American opinion in American affairs.

The Treaty was, on the Irish side, an act of submission to superior force.

It was a kind of compromise in principle in return for the gain of certain practical advantages. The reason for the submission was a judgment that the military effort of 1919-21, which brought Britain to the negotiating table, could not be sustained; that, if the British ultimatum of December 1921 was rejected, the Irish military position would collapse in the face of a British offensive of the kind that won it the war against the Boers twenty years earlier—the sweeping up of the populations of rebellious areas into concentration camps, and the establishment of a chain of military blockhouses around the country. The outcome of that would be reconquest and pacification on British terms.

That is the judgment which Collins acted upon, and his action established the framework of subsequent development. It is in the nature of a political judgment of that kind that the ground on which it is made cannot be demonstrated to be either true or false. There can be no testing of other possibilities. It might be that, if the British ultimatum had been defied, Lloyd George would have climbed down from his high horse. And, if he had set about making good his threat, it might be that re-conquest and pacification would have succeeded—or it might be that the Coalition would have fallen in the face of Irish defiance as it did less than a year later in the face of Turkish defiance.

It is not easy to think about the possibilities of that situation in this revisionist era because the revisionist mentality is utterly provincial in its outlook. Britain looms over it as if it was a gigantic fact of nature which it is useless to think about. It does not see Britain, and therefore the position of Britain in the world lies far beyond its wildest imaginings.

Britain engaged in multiple deceptions in its *"war that will end war"*. It deliberately destroyed three states—the German, Hapsburg and Ottoman Empires—throwing Central Europe and the Middle East into chaos. A fourth state, whose aggressive purposes it had encouraged in order to gain it as an ally—the Tsarist Empire—collapsed under the stress of war, giving rise to a new force which put a question mark over the political structure of the whole world. And Britain had not even won its great war of destruction by its own efforts. It ran out of money, and also out of productive capacity in the first year, and depended thereafter on loans from the United States. And, in the end, the United States had to go to war and defeat Germany in order to save its debtor from collapse. The British Empire therefore emerged from its freely chosen Great War as the greatest state the world had ever seen, but so indebted, so badly damaged, so demoralised, and having so many of its chickens coming home to roost, that it was no longer a functional world state. It lost the run of itself and it only needed one obstinate act of defiance to set an unravelling process in motion. Rejection of the Treaty ultimatum might have been that act. In the event, it was Attaturk's rebellion in the rump of the Ottoman state that caused the fall of the War Coalition and led to the shrinkage of the Imperial will. But the Irish 'settlement' probably prepared the way for the collapse—or, rather, the

Truce did. The Treaty was a partial recovery by Britain and does not bear O'Connor's interpretation of it. The demoralising event was the Truce—the implicit recognition by the Imperial State of belligerent rights for what had hitherto been described as a gang of cut-throats and assassins.

Revisionist historians suggest that the Treaty War was actually a civil war in fact as well as in name. Their notion is that Republican unity in 1919-21 was more apparent than real, that those who submitted to the British ultimatum had never really wanted an independent Republic, and that the ultimatum was the stimulus they needed to encourage them to take their stand on their own ground instead of being hustled along by the Republicans.

But the revisionists, who take the Treaty to be the origin of Irish democracy, never quote the Treatyites in support of their argument. Batt O'Connor's book should make it clear why they do not do so. It is evident that a desire to live under the sovereignty of the Crown played no part whatever in his decision to support the Treaty.

The Treatyites submitted to the threat of immediate and terrible war (or *"terrible and immediate war"* as Kevin O'Higgins put it) with the intention of zig-zagging back to the Republic as opportunities arose. And an earlier generation of historians did not attempt to conceal this fact.

Terence de Vere White, Anglo-Irish biographer of arch-Treatyite Kevin O'Higgins, wrote:

"Kevin O'Higgins, when he heard of a settlement, wrote a triumphant letter home to tell the news, but when the terms of the Treaty were disclosed, he expressed disappointment. This was the feeling of all Separatists. It must not be thought that there was a party who liked the terms in the ranks of the Republicans. There was not. But there was a sharp division as to the advisability of accepting or rejecting them" (*Kevin O'Higgins*, London, 1948, p65).

"it is clear that anyone who believed the Civil War was fought between ardent Republicans and loyal subjects of King George is making a great mistake" (p166).

Despite making the notorious statement that, "if we go into the Empire, we go in, not sliding in, not attempting to throw dust in our people's eyes, but we go in with our heads up", O'Higgins denied to the end that he had become an Imperialist. But I think he had. He was hijacked by the simplicity of his own logic. His remark about going into the Empire with our heads up was directed against what appeared to him to be the obscurantism of the position of De Valera's Document No. 2.

Much has been made in recent times of the fact that Dev read Machiavelli. It is suggested that this was a symptom of duplicity in the service of egoism. I take it for a sign that he understood that there is an irreducible element of obscurity in the human condition, and particularly in its political dimension, which must be manoeuvred around. I came to an appreciation of this in the course of investigating the relationship of Parliament and State in England, in connection with Lord Strafford around 1630 and Lord Clarendon in the early 1640s and Cromwell's floundering attempt to form a Parliamentary state. Dev apparently got at it through Machiavelli. Wherever he got it from, he had it. And the fact that he had it is what made all the difference between him and either Collins or O'Higgins.

Nevertheless O'Higgins, in his simple, brutal way, said things which make him unusable by the revisionist project of Anglicising Irish history.

A project is now afoot to make the Imperial ceremonies of Poppy Day an event in the official Irish Calendar. We are told that we have wilfully forgotten the 50,000 Irishmen who died for England in the Great War, and that the Irish must be jolted out of the unhealthy mental condition of being in denial about a big, indisputable fact like that. But the truth is that the Irish are being conned into a false memory of forgetting. The fact that 50,000 lives were lost gaining a victory for the British Empire, which it then proceeded to waste, was never forgotten. It was remembered, and regretted.

*

An Imperial remnant which had not supported the Republican development, but had no means of opposing it, attached itself to the Treaty cause, once the Treaty was signed and Sinn Fein began to split. Not having been part of the Republican unity, it could not in any substantial sense be a cause of the Treaty or the split, but it sought to benefit from the split and to roll back events towards the pre-1916 situation. As Eoin Neeson puts it:

> "Collins avowedly disliked politics and distrusted politicians. But he was too complex and intelligent a man to have believed 'the simple soldier' line with which he tried to impress others. Nevertheless he saw in politics and in politicians a threat to the dexterous net of intrigue which had woven and which he knew well how to manipulate. It may have been his fear of the solid-fronted politicians represented by De Valera... which helped him to turn towards Griffith—in reality so unlike him—and the prospect the latter offered of being a vehicle for the stepping stone theory. But in trying to make use of Griffith, Collins discovered when he returned having signed the Treaty that it was he who was being made use of. In trying to escape one set of politicians he fell head, neck and crop under the hooves of infinitely more dangerous, more subtle and more alien ones; who gave him the kind of support which masked a take-over-bid. That take-over-bid not alone had little or no place for the Stepping Stone, it represented a state of affairs to which Collins was fundamentally opposed" (*The Life And Death Of Michael Collins*, 1968, p68).

> "From the moment the split became public the powerful interests which

had been unfriendly or actively hostile towards the national movement during the period of its struggle with the British, began to make use of the new situation.

"They were the organs of power, other than recent political and military, in the country; the Church and the Press being the most important. With them however, must be included the banks, the influential groups which direct affairs and public opinion—the Free Masons, the Knights of Columbanus, the Southern Unionists, the non-aligned Protestants... Most of these had been bitterly opposed and hostile to Sinn Fein during the previous five years, the bitterness and hostility increasing with the success of Sinn Fein and the decline, as it were, in inverse ratio of their own influence in the land.

"Hitherto these elements were aligned in opposition to Sinn Fein and in support, to one degree or another, of what the British regime represented. This... was the only thing that they had in common in many instances; and in common they looked like losing all they stood for when Sinn Fein was successful—until the split made it possible for them to again participate effectively, *without having to come to terms with that which they had opposed so violently...*" (p64).

The civil institutions and conspiracies of Imperial Ireland, many of which were built up during the long era of the Penal Law system, lost their influence over the conduct of the populace when an independence party gave purposeful guidance to the democracy in the first election conducted on a democratic electoral franchise. The Treaty split presented them with the opportunity to regain influence by supporting the section which submitted to the British ultimatum.

Collins was unable to cope with the situation which his own decisive action in London on 6th December 1922 had brought about. He found himself supported by the power of money, by British guns, and by the influential connections of the old elite whose position he had brought close to collapse—supported and hustled and increasingly pinned down, as Gulliver was by the Lilliputians.

According to Batt O'Connor, he looked on Eoin O'Duffy as his heir. His actual heir proved to be Kevin O'Higgins. And the least that must be said is that O'Higgins did not betray his inheritance from Collins as much as he might have done. When the Imperial remnant felt strong enough to propose the building of a Great War Memorial in Merrion Square, he dismissed the proposal as follows:

"I believe that to devote Merrion Square to this purpose would be to give a wrong twist, as it were, a wrong suggestion to the origins of this state. It would be a falsehood, a falsehood by suppression of the truth and by a suggestion of something that is contrary to the truth... I say that any intelligent visitor, not particularly versed in the history of the country, would be entitled to conclude that the origins of this State, were connected... with the lives that were lost in France, Belgium, Gallipoli and so on. That is not the position. This State has other origins, and because it has other origins I do not wish to see it suggested, in stone or otherwise, that it has that origin.

"I want it to be understood that I speak in no spirit of hostility to ex-servicemen, *qua* ex-servicemen. Two members of my family served throughout that war—one who did not survive, in the British Army, and another who did in the Navy—and so it will be understood that it is no feeling of hostility to those who were through that war in the ranks of the British Army that I oppose this scheme; but this proposal, if it is proceeded with, means that you are to have here... a park monument dedicated to the memory of those men. I object to that because the fulfilment of such a project suggests that it is on that sacrifice that this State was reared... We have to go back a bit to get our perspective on this proposal. We have... to remember the political position of this country from about 1908... on to 1914...

"Then we narrowed on to the war situation of 1914. We had our talk of political dismemberment; we had our talk of partition; we had our conference on the less or more of partition; we had the shelving of the whole issue, the hanging up of the Bill until after the war, when that whole issue was to be reopened. The horse was to live and it would get grass after the war. The horse, not unwisely, as I see it, decided it would have a bid for grass before the end of the war. Somebody said, or wrote, that somehow, some time, and by somebody, revolutions must be begun. A revolution was begun in this country in Easter 1916. That revolution was endorsed by the people in a general election in 1918, and three years afterwards the representatives of the Irish people negotiated a Treaty with the British Government.

"...I submit to Deputies it is not wise to suggest that this State has any other origins than those. Let men think what they will of them; let men criticize them and hold their individual viewpoints, but those are the origins of the State. It would be lacking in a sense of truth, in a sense of historical perspective, a sense of symmetry to suggest that the State has not those origins, but that it is based in some way on the sacrifice of those who followed the advice of the parliamentary representatives of the day, and recruited in great numbers to the British Army to fight in the European War" (quoted from de Vere White, p170).

*

Collins's singular role in the war was to be the organiser of counter-intelligence and assassination in Dublin. The actual war was fought elsewhere, chiefly in Munster. Batt O'Connor, though a Kerryman, has nothing to tell about that. But counter-intelligence assassination was not the war, though it was necessary to the conduct of the war.

One of the most influential and neglected figures in Irish history since the Williamite conquest is Walter Cox, a gunsmith and United Irishman in the 1790s, and founder and publisher and, for the most part, author of the *Irish Magazine* from 1808 to 1812. In the latter capacity he created the modern Irish national movement, and he was, I think, largely responsible for weaning O'Connell off the leftovers of the Ascendancy nationalism of the late 18th century. In the former capacity he proposed to the United Irish leaders a policy which might have made that organisation effective in its conflict with the Ascendancy, but they rejected it.

What he proposed to them was that the terror tactics of the Ascendancy regime should be adopted by the United Irishmen and played back at the Ascendancy. He proposed targetted assassinations. Some members of the United Irish Directory saw that his proposal was realistic and relevant but they could not bring themselves to authorise it. They were idealistic gentry with ingrained chivalrous conceptions which disabled them for the task which they had set themselves. They would not do the dishonourable things that were necessary to survival and to victory, and so they saved their honour while their movement was destroyed by the terror of the unscrupulous regime.

Cox lived on to found the *Irish Magazine* in which he re-launched nationalism on a plebeian basis, deliberately discarding the modes of the gentry, and parting company with the gentry themselves, except for William Sampson (who is now even more forgotten than himself).

The singular role of Michael Collins in the Anglo-Irish War was to play the part scripted by Walter Cox a century and a quarter earlier—a part which it horrifies sensitive English souls to contemplate, but nevertheless a part which the English State has never been short of people to perform.

The British State is capacious enough to encompass the extremes of both squeamishness and unscrupulousness. It ensures the good conscience of its unscrupulous agents while allowing the squeamish to indulge their own consciences to their heart's content, fostering a kind of rhetoric in the public mind which allows each its autonomy and its appropriate ignorance of the other. The two exist in close conjunction only in the depths of Whitehall. Britain is a well set-up state. Heinrich Himmler admired it. He aspired to do dreadful things in what he conceived to be the interest of the German people while leaving the German people themselves in a state of innocence, as his English models were accustomed to do. And who can say that, if Germany had won the War, the German genocide would not now be as little heard of as the English genocides are, and the German people would not be experiencing the sense of well-being which the English have habitually experienced over the centuries of warfare and atrocity by which their state provided for them?

This is an unpleasant aspect of the kind of modern human existence of which the English state itself is the chief architect. The English state does not encourage its people to dwell on it, but brushes it under the carpet. It is able to brush it under the carpet because it managed to end up on the winning side of all the wars it instigated. And, in my view, brushing it under the carpet was the right thing to do with it. But what is utterly repulsive is the modern English practice of humiliating and perverting those whom it has defeated by rubbing their noses in the atrocious aspect of their conduct.

The Irish were not defeated in 1921, and in the 1930s they regained much of what had been conceded in 1921. But, over the past quarter century, they have been allowing themselves to be treated as if they had been defeated. That is the only meaning I can find in what is called 'revisionism'. The Oxford University Press is rehashing the British propaganda of the Black-and-Tan war and the Irish Universities are accepting the confection as the history of Ireland for that period.

A book on the IRA in Cork was published by the Clarendon Press a few years ago. Those who fought in 1919-21 to give effect to the electoral mandate of 1918 are described as serial murderers with a bent for genocide. The History Department of Cork University arranged a meeting to be addressed by the author. Uncritical praise was heaped on him. There was only one dissenter at the meeting. When he began to speak, the academic mob tried to howl him down. Prominent in the mob was a lecturer called Bielenberg, whose father had been a dissenter in Germany under Hitler. But I suppose that's the way of the world. I learned from Samuel Butler that generations tend to go by contraries.

There was an unpleasant aspect to the Anglo-Irish War on its Irish side. If it is to be raked over, then so must the unpleasantness on the other side—the side which made it necessary that a war should be fought to give effect to an election result. And, on that other side, if one applies the democratic standard, there is nothing to be found but unpleasantness.

Collins tended to that aspect of the War. De Valera distanced himself from it while taking responsibility for it, and because of that he has in recent years been criticised as a hypocrite. It was hypocrisy only if one describes the modern state as a hypocrisy.

De Valera engaged in open warfare in 1916. Then he became political leader of the state based on the 1918 election, while Collins tended to another aspect of the matter. But Collins, the assassin, is more acceptable to the revisionists—he is more usable for their purposes—than De Valera. And so we get De Valera being condemned as a hypocrite because at the outset he developed the division of functions which is found in all modern states, instead of behaving like a clan chief, or as a mediaeval king in whose person all functions are fused together.

Tim Pat Coogan has played a curious role in all of this. He was editor of the *Irish Press* in the 1970s. *The Irish Press*, founded by De Valera, was the Fianna Fail newspaper. I heard Coogan on Radio Eireann some years ago explaining that he had broken the alignment between the *Irish Press* and Fianna Fail, and assuming it to be self-evident that that was a good thing, even though modern democracy is necessarily party-political. The outcome is that Fianna Fail became a party without a journalistic organ. But it remains the major party of the state even though the whole journalism of the state is directed against it, which is not an arrangement conducive to robust political health in the state.

Having been the Fine Gael editor of the Fianna Fail newspaper, Coogan went on to write much-publicised books on Collins and De Valera, in which Collins is depicted as a heroic figure and De Valera is systematically denigrated as a malevolent egoist. At a moment when the welfare of the body politic needed an understanding of the Treaty War which transcended the passions generated by the Treaty split and enabled the event to become a source of general experience, Coogan leaped back over sixty years, stirring up the passions of 1922 as if the subsequent development had not happened.

Coogan's Collins offensive provoked a remarkable counter-offensive in the form of a small book by Michael O Cuinneagain, *On The Arm Of Time*. This was published by O Cuinneagain himself (at Tantallon, Donegal Town) and received no publicity, even though it easily surpasses Coogan in intellectual force. (Coogan's strong point is industriousness.)

O Cuinneagain maintains that Collins was disabled by blackmail at a critical juncture in the London negotiations, and that it was under the pressure of blackmail that he signed the Treaty and browbeat the others into signing it. The blackmail was conducted at the London residence of Lady Lavery. Its instrument was Moya Llewelyn Davies. Moya Llewelyn Davies was the wife of Crompton Llewelyn Davies, an associate of Lloyd George who had held a number of minor positions in the administration. Earlier in life—or in an earlier life—she had been Moya O'Connor of Dublin. She was closely acquainted with Collins in the Gaelic League in London before the War and her son was his son. She turned up at Lady Lavery's residence on the evening when Collins was there deciding how to respond to Lloyd George's ultimatum, and her presence, with the implicit threat of exposure over his illegitimate son, was the clincher.

We are here in the region of conspiracy theories. But few things in political affairs are more absurd than the assumption that conspiracy theories are false. The effectiveness of the British State over the centuries has had much to do with its competence in the business of conspiracy. The very Reformation in which the modern English state and society originate was much more a product of conspiracy than of the flow of religious feeling. Elizabeth's chief minister, Cecil, was a spy-master. And blackmail was always the small change of its Irish administration.

I am not suggesting that O Cuinneagain is right. But I followed up some of the things he says and I could not find that he was wrong. The matter is too complex to summarise here, except to say that I have always found Collins's conduct from December 1921 onwards very puzzling, and Coogan does not resolve the puzzle.

Moya Llewelyn Davies was one of five children in a middle-class nationalist family in Blackrock, four of whom died, along with their mother, from eating contaminated mussels gathered at Monkstown beach: an incident which is mentioned in *Ulysses*. Her husband, who was much older, was the son of an Anglican clergyman of the 'Christian Socialist' tendency founded by F.D. Maurice (which was a strand in the popular Imperialism of the generation leading up to 1914), and was himself a member of Lloyd George's entourage in the radical Liberal tendency—and Lloyd George, of course, became the ultimate British Imperialist in the course of the Great War, the collapse of his Coalition in 1922 marking the beginning of the decline of the Empire.

Moya's son, who is alleged to be Collins's, was born in 1912. He became a very influential writer on architecture, held the Chair of Architecture at London University, planned the new town of Milton Keynes, and was made a Life Per in 1963. (And by a curious coincidence there is currently in print a work entitled, *The Use Of Density In Urban Planning*, DETR, June 1998, the authors being "Llewelyn-Davies, Consultants, and Michael Collins".)

Moya's husband held the position of Solicitor General to the Post Office in Lloyd George's administration and was responsible for the censorship of the mails, but was obliged to resign during the Anglo-Irish war when a raid in Dublin uncovered evidence that Moya was involved to some extent in Collins's activities, and she was imprisoned briefly.

Moya herself translated Maurice O'Sullivan's *Twenty Years A-Growing* with George Thomson, the translation being published in 1953.

According to O Cuinneagain: "Moya was ghost writer for Bat O'Connor's book…, and for Charles Dalton's book, *'With The Dublin Brigade'*". Both of these books were published in London by Peter Davies in 1929. Dalton's book has an odd structure. It begins with a 25-page historical Introduction, *followed* by an *"Author's Preface"*, which suggests that the Author did not write the Introduction. And some formulations in the Introduction, especially on the Treaty, are very similar to those in O'Connor's book.

Tim Pat Coogan: says

> "Moya, who had helped Batt O'Connor with the publication of his book on Collins, showed the manuscript of her autobiography to Batt and his wife. Mrs. O'Connor was aghast to read her account of the relationship with Collins and decided something must be done. She summoned some of his closest associates, including Liam Tobin and Frank Thornton, to a reading. It was generally agreed that the book contained material concerning their dead leader that should not be printed. They decided to send the unfortunate Moya an anonymous death threat. The crude censorship worked, the book never appeared and the manuscript has been lost sight of' (*Michael Collins*, 1991 edn., p285-6. Coogan's source is O'Connor's daughter, Sister Margaret Mary, a Poor Clare nun).

What we have in the present book, then, is Batt O'Connor's story, told with the help of Moya Llewelyn Davies, who was a hero-worshipper of Collins. It is somewhat streamlined. Letters written by O'Connor at the time—which are not included here—show that his acceptance of the Treaty was not quite as matter of fact as it is represented in his book and that the barbs against De Valera do not express his attitude to Dev as it was before the Treaty split. The book is a Treatyite document published quite late in the day, when the Free State Government had become active in the affairs of the Empire. It is therefore all the more convincing as evidence that the Republican unity of 1919-21 was not an illusory appearance covering a section whose real object was self-government under the Crown within the Empire.

Those who submitted to the British ultimatum in December 1921 had fought for the 1919 Republic no less than those who refused to submit. Insofar as some general ground of division can be found as determining who went which way in the Treaty split, it was not in the difference between those who wanted independent government and those who did not, nor in a difference between those who were democratic in outlook and those who were not, but in a difference between the pre-democratic Republican elite of the IRB and those who were gripped by the democratic enthusiasm of 1918.

The IRB did not proceed by democratic methods because its aim of establishing an independent state in Ireland was not democratically achievable. Ireland was made part of the British state by right of conquest, the operative conquest being that of 1690. The Irish were entirely excluded from political life in Ireland for over a century, and were substantially excluded for a century and a half. They were readmitted in the middle of the 19th century on condition that Ireland was an inseparable part of the British State and Empire. It was around this time that the British state began to use the language of democracy. Before this time it had been explicitly anti-democratic. The long war against France (1793-1815) was a war against democracy, preached as such by Edmund Burke. But the old regime of the Glorious Revolution of 1688 was infected by the democracy that it fought against and democratisation began in 1832. Although the electorate was a small proportion of the adult population until 1918, the state began to describe itself as a democracy. The Irish were free to play a part in the elite democracy of the British state, but only on condition that they operated within the parameters of British political life. This was made abundantly clear when an Irish national-democratic movement was launched in the 1840s—the Young Ireland movement. The Young Ireland leaders were arrested, tried and convicted for publishing national-democratic propaganda in which the restriction imposed on Irish political life by the British state was held to be undemocratic and therefore not morally binding.

The Irish Republican Brotherhood was organised as a conspiracy in the years following the dispersal of the Young Ireland movement.

Conspiracy and democracy are different modes of operation. I suppose that it is conceivable that a conspiracy might be so extensive that it is a virtual democracy, nevertheless it differs from democracy in being a form of covert activity which conceals itself from the state.

It was possible in relatively lax Continental states for conspiracies to be organised very extensively. That was not possible in Ireland, where the country was honeycombed by the British apparatus of espionage and informal coercion. The IRB conspiracy was easily penetrated and disrupted by the British state. The Fenian Rising of 1867 was a sad affair, considered as a particular event, but it generated a widespread sentiment of independence amongst the populace.

The IRB survived as an organisation by moving to the United States when it was suppressed in Ireland. And the state which suppressed the Fenian conspiracy provided a safe haven in England for Mazzini's Italian nationalist conspiracy. The middle-class democracy which was national democratic in much of its Continental foreign policy was totalitarian and imperialist in its dealings with the malcontent nationality at home.

(Mazzini published terrorist propaganda in London against the established authorities in Italy. He had reasons of prudence for not associating himself with the nationalist agitation in Ireland which was directed against the state which was giving him a safe haven. His politic silence on the Young Ireland and Fenian movements, and some private thoughts attributed to him after his death, were adduced by Professor Nicholas Mansergh, and more strongly by Professor Roy Foster, as influential evidence that Irish nationality was not authentic. In this they only continue the duplicity of the British state of Mazzini's time which supported abroad what it punished at home. But I notice that Brian Feeney, who should know better, echoes Professor Foster in his history of Sinn Fein: "Young Ireland was modelled on the Young Italy movement of Guiseppi Mazzini... Unfortunately for his Irish disciples, Mazzini did not believe Ireland qualified for independence. He did not think it had a culture distinct from England" (*Sinn Fein: A Hundred Turbulent Years*, p21. The writers of *The Nation* were bred under the massive influence of O'Connell, who had been working up national sentiment for a decade before their arrival. Italy had no equivalent of O'Connell. And I do not know of any evidence that *The Nation* group were 'disciples' of Mazzini.)

The British state, which for a couple of generations had purported to be a democracy, became a democracy in 1918. The 1918 Reform Act tripled the electorate. This was the greatest enfranchising measure in the history of the British state, yet it is rarely mentioned. There is frequent reference to the Reform Acts of 1832 and 1867, but I have never seen a reference to the 1918 Reform Act.

Britain might be described as democratic in the late 19th century if classical Athens is taken for the prototype of democracy. Democratic Athens was a slave state. Democracy was an activity of the leisured classes. In Britain before 1918 it was an activity of middle-class men and upper working-class men. In 1918 all men and most women were admitted to it in conditions of very great popular excitement. The outcome of the 1918 Election in Ireland would probably have been very different if the Election had been held on the 1910 franchise, and without the preceding upheaval of the Conscription Crisis. The Anglicising historians prowl around that fact sniffing it like a cat around a bowl of hot porridge. They feel that the actual election result can be invalidated by use of it, but they can not quite figure out how to do it. It is problematical—as problematical as it was for the Castle propagandist Major Street in 1920: How on the one hand to appear as democrats against the Republicans and on the other to blame Republicanism on democracy.

"Vous l'avez voulu, Georges Dardin" is the best comment on it. "This is what you wanted, George Dardin" (the refrain of a Moliere play). Britain outwitted itself by making its Imperialistic war on Germany a war for democracy and the rights of small nations. Its advocacy of national democracy was for export only, as in Mazzini's time, but it struck root at home. But it *said* it wanted democracy and the rights of small nations to be established in the world, and the Irish took it at its word.

The Treaty split might be described as a parting of the ways between the Republicans of the pre-1914 era—who never for a moment believed that the British state had become a convert to democracy and the rights of small nations and that independence was to be got by voting for it—and those who were stirred to democratic action by British conduct in the Great War, including the democratic propaganda which was such a major element in that conduct.

The Anglicising historians repeatedly assert that the conspiratorial Republicans played a crucial part in the reconstruction of Sinn Fein in 1917-18 and in the selection of candidates for the Election, and they take that to be a fact which detracts from the democratic force of the electoral mandate. But those same historians look to the 1922 Election as the originating event of Irish democracy, choosing to overlook the fact that it was the conspirators of 1918 who were in command of the 1922 election—and were much more overtly and manipulatively in command than in 1918.

In fact one of these historians concedes the point. Professor Garvin of University College, Dublin, in the book in which he argues that Irish democracy began in the 1922 Election, says:

"Irish democracy was founded by unenthusiastic and rather authoritarian democrats (*1922: The Birth Of Irish Democracy*, 062).

It seems to me to be a misapplication of the term 'democracy' to apply it to any of the contending forces in an authoritarian state, and to be an exceptionally gross misapplication when the matter at issue is entirely the product of the authoritarian state.

The British state did not cease to be authoritarian in Ireland with the 1918 democratisation of the franchise. Indeed, it became more generally, more overtly,and more forcibly authoritarian than it had been for generations. By denying to the Irish the very thing they had voted for, it perpetuated the authoritarianism of the pre-democratic era into the democratic era—and the authoritarianism became more active than it had any need to be in the pre-democratic era, when the expectations of the populace had been kept at a low level.

Democratic politics are the function of a freely operating state, in which the coercive pressure of a state apparatus, whether external or domestic, is not brought to bear on determining the outcome of elections. That was the test applied by the British to enemy states at the time of the Great War, and it is the test which it applies today to countries like Serbia and Zimbabwe. It is therefore a test which may be reasonably applied to Irish political affairs under British rule up to 1921, and under British hegemony for some time subsequent to 1921. The 1922 Election does not emerge as a democratic event from the application of that test.

Treatyites and anti-Treatyites were not divided over the kind of state they wanted. Both sides wanted the independent republic which the electorate had voted for. The war to impose the Treaty is therefore not properly described when it is called a civil war.

The IRB politicians, whose Republicanism was not the product of the democratic enthusiasm generated by British conduct in the Great War, did not believe that Britain had become a democratic state. They engaged in electoral activity as a propaganda tactic in the long conflict with the authoritarian state. In the event, they treated the elections as demonstrations of protest which might induce Britain to concede a bit more than it would otherwise have done, and they were willing to do a deal that fell well short of the electoral mandate. But those who had become active Republicans under the influence of the Great War, when it appeared that Britain had committed itself to democracy and the rights of small nations, did not find it easy to shrug off all of that and go along with the *realpolitik* approach of the conspirators.

It seems to me that that, roughly, was the ground of division over the Treaty. And it explains why Batt O'Connor found that people who were timid at the time of the 1916 Insurrection rejected the Treaty.

*

O'Connor relates the story of a Christmas dinner given by Collins to four of his colleagues in 1920 at the Gresham Hotel, where they were surrounded by a company of Auxiliaries, and talked their way out of it even though the Auxiliaries had a photo of Collins, and they found in his pocket a notebook in which he had written a note about rifles. Coogan (page 165) also relates this incident, but with the additional detail that Collins was separated from the others and taken to the toilets for individual questioning.

O Cuinneagain comments:

"On the same day, 24th December 1920, the Police Gazette, *Hue and Cry*, published, among others, a photograph of Collins which made him readily recognisable to any officer. This disclosure casts grave doubt on some of the stories told about Collins and his alleged 'miraculous' escapes... In view of the photograph in the Gazette, published that day, it is difficult to accept that the Auxiliaries did not recognise Collins under a bright light in the toilet" (p19).

O Cuinneagain suggests that Collins had an equivocal relationship with the British Government through Lloyd George's special representative, Alfred Cope; that there was never a price on his head during the Anglo-Irish War; that, far from being reluctant to go on the delegation in the Autumn of 1921, he was insistent; and that he had De Valera's telephone calls monitored.

I can offer no opinion on these things. Collins may well have had an ambiguous relationship with Dublin Castle. So had Walter Cox in 1798. If he had, it was presumably for an IRB purpose, and in accordance with an IRB assumption that British democracy was a mere illusion with regard to Irish affairs and that a compromise with the brute power of the Empire was inevitable sooner or later. This would suggest that he adopted the Stepping Stones approach long before taking affairs into his own hands in December 1921. And I do not intend to inform myself better so that I can form an opinion. The reason is not that I am predisposed towards scepticism about conspiracy theories but that, in the course of a quarter of a century during which I held an off-beat political position in Belfast, I came to take it for granted that British political life operated in a maze of conspiracies.

British conspiratorial activity with the object of engineering malleable public opinion in the North came to nothing because the raw antagonism of the Protestant and Catholic communities was preserved intact by the perverse mode of government that Britain chose to establish in the Six Counties when it was partitioning the country. Northern Ireland was excluded from the political life of the British state, and its mode of government consisted of little more than the policing of the Catholic community by the Protestant community and the waving of Union Jacks. I discussed this with many British politicians. All agreed in private that the system was perverse, and that its operation preserved and aggravated the antagonism of the communities. This was something that no experienced British politician could ever have failed to see. Why, then, was it established? And why was it maintained after its effects became obvious?

Why was the Catholic community, after it was cut off from the national state, excluded from the possibility of participation in the political life of the British state? Because Northern Ireland had a purpose beyond itself. Its purpose was not good government in the Six Counties. Its purpose was to give Whitehall leverage on the part of Ireland that was escaping from it. That purpose was undeclared, and undeclarable. It was nevertheless a definite purpose, and was obstinately persisted in regardless of its consequences within Northern Ireland.

(It was half-declared by Churchill in February 1925 when, as Chancellor of the Exchequer, he was defending an irregular financial measure relating to Northern Ireland against a Labour Party which had not yet been properly initiated into the understanding of the matter. These vital understandings—these secrets of state—are not comprehensively worked out and then covered by the Official Secrets Act. No secrets could be kept that way. Kipling explained the English way of these things:

"Being void of self-expression they confide their views to none;
But sometimes in the smoking-room one learns why things were done
Yes, sometimes in the smoking-room through clouds of 'Ers' and 'Ums'
Obliquely and by inference illumination comes,
Of some step that they have taken, or some action they approve,
Embellished by the argot of the Upper Fourth Remove".)

I spent many years going over the sequence of events through which the First World War came about before concluding that it was intelligible only on the assumption of deliberate British manipulation of the conflicts and ambitions of Continental states since the Boer War. France, the traditional enemy, had been shackled. The Russian threat to the British frontier on the other side of the world had been contained by Britain's new ally, Imperialist Japan. A new state had arisen in Europe, Germany. Its rapid industrial development made it the first European economic rival of Britain, and its foreign policy of supporting the continuing existence of the older states in the world conflicted with the expansionist ambitions of the British Empire, particularly in the Middle East. The First World War was a war to destroy Germany as an economic rival and an obstacle to the open-ended expansion of the British Empire. It began when the Kaiser sent a message of support to the Boer Republics when Britain was about to make war on them. Preparations for the war on Germany were set in motion very soon after the South African matter had been settled. France and Russia were taken off the enemy list and their ambitions were encouraged to direct themselves towards Germany. And the German Government never suspected that it had been marked down in Whitehall as Britain's primary enemy until Britain declared war on it a moment after it became engaged in a war on two fronts with Russia and France. (The Russian Army alone was bigger than the German, and the French was roughly equal. The British intervention stopped German trade by sea, and added Japan and Italy to the Allied combination, which had been greatly superior from the start.)

That was one of the most outstanding diplomatic achievements in recorded history. It was accomplished by informal understandings amongst the small public school elite which controlled the Foreign Office and the Army—the elite which communicated in *"the argot of the Upper Fourth Remove"*. Perhaps some documentary evidence of it might have been found if the Foreign Office archives had fallen suddenly into enemy hands. As it was, I never expected to see any explicit evidence of it from the horse's mouth. But then I learned from Pat Walsh that an American Ambassador in London, Henry White, had recorded the following conversation with Arthur Balfour in 1910:

> "Balfour: We are probably fools not to find a reason for declaring war on Germany before she builds too many ships and takes away our trade.
>
> "White: You are a very high-minded man in private life. How can you possibly contemplate anything so politically immoral as provoking a war against a harmless nation which has as good a right to a navy as you have? If you wish to compete with German trade, work harder.
>
> "Balfour: That would mean lowering our standard of living. Perhaps it would be simpler for us to have a war.
>
> "White: I am shocked that you of all men should enunciate such principles.
>
> "Balfour: Is it a question of right or wrong? Maybe it is just a question of keeping our supremacy" (Henry White and Allan Nevins, *Thirty*

Years Of American Diplomacy, 1937, p257, quoted in *The Rise And Fall Of Imperial Ireland* by Pat Walsh, 2003, p524).

Balfour was an intellectual as well as a politician—indeed, a philosopher rather than an intellectual. He was born into the magic circle. He was Irish Secretary under the Prime Ministership of his uncle, Lord Salisbury, and he made a remarkable tour of the west of Ireland which led him to conclude that the farmers would make better landowners than the landlords. And it was under his own Prime Ministership that land ownership was transferred to the farmers. He was also Bloody Balfour, who suppressed land agitation as a preliminary to reform. A generation ago he was still remembered by old men in Donegal, even though not a single book about him has ever been published by an Irish historian.

He was a member of the Imperial administration which won the Boer War by means of destroying the crops of Boer farmers, sweeping up the population into Concentration Camps in which 26,000 women and children died in a few months, and covering the country with a chain of blockhouses—the methods which Lloyd George was understood to mean by his threat of terrible and immediate war.

And he went on to become Foreign Secretary in the Coalition in the Great War.

Arthur Balfour knew what was what in British affairs. But he was untypical in a particular way. He did not communicate in *"the argot of the Upper Fourth Remove"*. He was a kind of belated flowering of the Scottish Enlightenment at the heart of the British power structure. And that is why we have got this frank explanation of what it was all about.

The State that could imagine and carry through that project against Germany is certainly capable of establishing a disorderly structure of government in the Six Counties, and enduring the decades of disorder, for the purpose of retaining leverage on the 26 Counties. That is what it did in fact, and I was driven to the conclusion that it was doing it deliberately. The alternative explanation is that it somehow did not know what it was doing, that it did not see what a strange and unnatural Constitutional entity Northern Ireland was, and that the leverage which Whitehall actually got on political and cultural affairs in the Republic as a consequence of the disorder in the North was not intended, but happened blind. And I found that incredible.

It was not as an anti-Partitionist that I reached these conclusions. My time in Belfast was not spent in anti-Partition agitation, but in attempting to incorporate the North into the democratic political life of the British state. I spent about a quarter of a century in that attempt, along with Jack Lane. We helped to defend West Belfast against the Unionist pogrom of August 1969 before going against the stream of nationalist opinion with the project of dissolving Northern Ireland into the democratic life of the British state—and discovering that the corridors of power in Whitehall were unalterably opposed to that project, even though it was admitted that it offered the best prospect for peace and normality in the Six Counties. If our purpose had been simply anti-Partitionist, I doubt that we would have come to see the British State as clearly as we did.

In the light of this experience I can only see Batt O'Connor's reflections on the North—and how there would have been Irish unity but for the 'Civil War'—as simple-minded. He has little understanding either of Ulster Unionism or the British state. But that does not make him unique.

I do not share Michael O Cuinneagain's vantage point, but I am entirely in agreement with him when he says:

> "The lack of genuine research which might take a little of the glitter away from Collins' record has been very apparent. Most writers attempt to use Collins to denigrate de Valera's role in Irish political life. There appears to be a campaign, an organised and orchestrated campaign, to belittle de Valera and his contribution to events in 1921/22, and by implication his subsequent achievements in Government" (p24).

At a moment when the 'Civil War' needed to be understood from a more general viewpoint than was available to any of the participants at the time, it was re-activated ideologically with the object of eroding the whole independence movement. Coogan indulged in a blind adulation of Collins and demonisation of Dev from a very narrow, though vigorous, nationalist impulse. Others sought to use Collins for a very different purpose than Coogan but his wild flailings eased their way.

Batt O'Connor's memoir predates the complicating development in which De Valera led the Free State to independence and a Government led by Treatyites declared it to be a Republic and ended its association with the British Empire and Commonwealh. What it represents is Collins as the simple soldier conducting the counter-intelligence dimension of the war. Collins, the mastermind of the IRB, was far from being a simple soldier. But that is the facet which he presented to Batt O'Connor.

The first half of this book is about O'Connor himself. I think it is the more interesting part.

Following O'Connor's memoir, Mrs. Batt O'Connor's recollections, which she lodged in the Bureau of Military History, are reproduced. They appear in print for the first time and give further brief insights into the events related by her husband. The details provided in the Bureau records list Mrs. O'Connor's contribution as follows:

Document No. **W.S. 330.**	**Identity**
Witness	Member of Gaelic League, 1913-
Mrs. Batt O'Connor,	**Subject**
37 Eglington Road,	Meetings of Irish Volunteer leaders at her home, Dublin
File No. S.1456	and other incidents of national interest 1913-1921

Brendan Clifford
March 2004

With Michael Collins In The Fight For Irish Independence

by
Batt O'Connor, TD

Introduction

In East Kerry, adjacent to the bounds of three counties—Kerry, Cork and Limerick—is the ancient village of Brosna. It dates back to the days of St. Mollang, the patron saint of the district. Here I was born on the 4th of July 1870.

I was educated at the local thatched National School. It was a mixed school of boys and girls, of which there were about 200. In summer time and on fine days all the junior classes were taught out of doors.

When I left school at the age of seventeen I went work with my father and elder brother to learn the trade of stonemason. I took great pride in the trade of masonry, and felt quite a man when I was taught the mason's language, which is well guarded within the trade. Handymen, or those who cannot lay claim to be inheritors of the craft on the father's or the mother's side, are not supposed to be allowed into the secret knowledge of the language.

At the age of twenty-three I went to America. I set sail in October 1893. My sorrow was great at having to part from my mother whom I dearly loved, as I was loved equally fondly by her. There were five other children younger than myself; and in losing me my poor mother felt that her chief prop was gone. But I told her to keep up her heart for I would be able to help her, so far as money went, even better than before, and I faithfully kept my promise.

When I landed in Boston I was met on the wharf by the best and most affectionate cousin that it was ever the lot of an emigrant to be blessed with— my cousin, Tom James O'Connor. He had a boot-and-shoe store in Manchester, New Hampshire. We went that Sunday evening to my sister's house in East Spruce Street, Manchester, and never shall I forget my welcome. They could not make enough of me or tire of hearing all my news of home. We made a merry night of it.

Not being a fully-fledged bricklayer, I took up work as a stonemason, and I got my first job building a new Catholic church in a small town, Berlin Falls, in the northern part of the state of New Hampshire. I worked there till 1894 when I returned to Manchester for Thanksgiving, and enjoyed a good night's fun at the Sheridan's Ball in the Mechanics Hall.

I was fully employed all the time I was in America, and improved very much at my trade, especially in bricklaying; but I found life very strenuous. We worked at least twice as hard as I was accustomed to do in Ireland. The Summers there are very warm, and I often longed for home, with the mild climate and easy way of living. I was never able to imagine myself settling down in America. The call of Ireland was always very strong in my nature. I wrote home unfailingly once a month, and all the time I was away I received a weekly newspaper from my native Kerry.

In this way my thoughts were constantly kept in touch with home, and after five years I returned to Ireland, landing at Cobh (then called Queenstown) on a beautiful evening in August 1898. I hurried home to see all those whom I loved in Brosna, and, after a week of perfect happiness, I returned to Cobh, where I worked on a brick building which was being erected on Spike Island. Here I worked at somewhat the rate of speed in laying bricks which I had acquired in America, but this was far in excess of what my fellow-workmen were accustomed to, and a bad feeling arose which ended with the whole fourteen bricklayers refusing to work with me any more. So I told my employer to pay me whatever I had earned; as I had no wish to be the cause of any trouble in his business.

After another visit home to Brosna I took train for Dublin, where I arrived at 7.30 in the evening. Next morning I went to look around the City. This was my first visit to the Capital, and I had not a friend or acquaintance in the place, but my few years spent in America had given me self-confidence, and I was quite accustomed to being a stranger in a strange town. I was at once delighted with the appearance of the City—it was of such stately, ancient design, so different from what I had seen in America. My heart warmed to it, with its cut stone buildings of beautiful architecture and perfect workmanship. The people, too, were so charming, so friendly, and so willing to show the lay of their city to a stranger.

The more I saw of Dublin the more loth I was to leave it, so that I made enquiries as to what prospects there were in the building trade. I was told they were good. The link line connecting the North Wall with Kingsbridge was being built, and a Power House was being constructed at Ringsend for the electrifying of the trams.

I applied for work at the Power House, and started laying bricks on the following morning. I was delighted with the manner and disposition of the Dublin bricklayer. I found him also a first-class mechanic, with an all-round knowledge of his trade, so different from the American who specializes in one branch and knows scarcely anything of the other parts of his trade.

It was the month of November when I came to Dublin, and at Christmas, joyfully, I went home to Brosna, to spend it with my mother, and with the girl to whom I was engaged to be married. I told my sweetheart all about Dublin. I said it was just the place I would love to settle down in, and she agreed that we would get married at Easter.

I returned to Dublin after spending the happiest Christmas of my life. Easter was not long delayed. I went down for my wedding and brought back my wife to the new home I had prepared for her. Within a year I had launched out as a sub-contractor, doing the brickwork on contract in the building of a terrace of houses in Kilmainham, and afterwards in Anglesea Road.

It was now the year 1900. I had begun to save money and had decided that the time had come for me to strike out on my own as a speculative builder. My capital was small, and during the first couple of years I had many anxious times, but by hard work and the goodness of God I surmounted my difficulties. I built houses in Anglesea Road, in Dolphin's Barn, and in Eglinton Road, Donnybrook, all of which I sold for good prices—all but one house in Eglinton Road which I let for rent, and which is my present residence.

I also built twelve houses in Brendan Road, Donnybrook, which I still own. The road was virgin soil when I started to put houses on it and had not yet received a name. The ground landlord suggested several titles, all of them copied from streets in London. To this I objected, contending that it should be called by a name associated with Ireland. I suggested St. Brendan Road, but "Saint" was objectionable to his Protestant susceptibilities. So we compromised. I surrendered "Saint" in exchange for his London title, and the road became Brendan Road. I have mentioned this incident because No. 1 Brendan Road was my home for many years, and beneath its roof found shelter some of the bravest men who fought in the Irish Revolution.

CHAPTER I
First Steps In Patriotism

Like most Irishmen who were born in a country village, I had seen in my childhood the poverty and sufferings of our people under alien rule.

The national spirit in Brosna was good. We had evictions, and raids by bailiffs who seized the people's cattle when they could not pay the rent. Very often there were reprisals. We had boycotting and *"moonlighting"*, and I remember a Company of cavalry—The Scots Greys—being brought into Brosna to protect a bailiff who was about to give evidence against some prisoners. A young girl from the district was sent to prison for assaulting this bailiff, who had been employed to dispossess the farmer for whom she worked. A farmer was imprisoned for upholding the principles of the Land League, and his neighbours planted his crops and saved his small harvest for his family.

The emigration from our district was continuous. I had seen young men and women going away, amid terrible heartbreaking scenes of farewell, to earn a living for themselves in America, and to send money home to help their parents. I myself had been one of those emigrants and I carried away those pictures with me.

To leave Ireland does not make one love Ireland more, but it does make one aware of the strength of that love. While we are at home, Ireland is a part of ourselves. Its landscape is as familiar as the face of father or mother. We take it for granted, and are not conscious of the strong hold it has upon us. But when we are withdrawn from the familiar horizon and find ourselves in a new setting, we realize that however fine and splendid it is, it is not home. It has no associations. In America I was often lonely for the old scenes. I would recall places where I played and romped as a child. I would think of the Irish voices and Irish phrases which I did not notice at all when I was at home—the *"God bless you"* and *"God save you"* which the Irish who go to America learn to be ashamed to say any more. I would try to recall the smell of the turf, and I would think of the streams in which I went fishing, and the places where I had found a bird's nest; and I longed to see them all again. There were times when I would yearn even for the bareness and narrow limits of my old home.

In the second year I was in America I saw a St. Patrick's Day parade in Providence, Rhode Island. I walked in the procession, and in the emotion I felt, walking as one of that vast crowd of Irish emigrants celebrating our national festival, I awoke to the full consciousness of my love for my country. That awakening was one of the forces bringing me home, and it led me inevitably to the day when I joined the Gaelic League two years after my return, and to another memorable occasion when, a few years later, I took my oath to the Irish Republican Brotherhood by the graveside of Wolfe Tone.

At first, on coming home, I had been disappointed at what had seemed to me the apathy of my countrymen for the old Cause. I know now that in forming that opinion I was judging by appearances. I was not looking below the surface. After events helped to enlighten me. When the big situation came it was the Irish at home who rose to it. Once their imaginations were stirred by the sacrifice of a few brave men, they played their parts nobly in the war which followed, risking their lives and their homes. The Irish in America sent home money generously for that fight, but when Michael Collins said: *"It is not so much your subscriptions I want. Will you send me a thousand fighting men?"* only a few responded to his appeal.

It is easy for exiles in America to wave flags and sing the old patriotic songs. It is not only easy but satisfying. When I walked in the procession I have spoken of, I felt I was a great Irishman, that we were making a fine gesture to the foreigners among whom we lived. In America we were well fed, our livelihood was safe. We were in a free country. In raising our banners and giving a few dollars to one of the Irish organizations we felt we were doing great things for our motherland. But at home our time was all taken up with the business of getting enough bread and butter. We did not need parades to remind us of Ireland and our lost liberty. We were too near the reality of the situation. Only a few had the leisure and the spirit to think of the old Cause, and they thought of it seriously as something which must be fought for and suffered for.

There was another reason for the apparent apathy and indifference. The Irish Parliamentary Party still controlled the country, and their policy of looking to England for everything was destroying the national pride. The people had got into the way of looking not so much for freedom, as for doles, which their representatives were to coax for them out of the British Government.

Our national self-respect was at a very low ebb. When we lost our Dublin Parliament, and Irish representatives began to go over to the London House of Commons, the English won a great victory over us. But we gave them at least as great a victory when we began to speak their language at their bidding and became ashamed of our own. Whatever we wanted to do in Ireland we had first to get permission from England, and, to earn a livelihood, a knowledge of the Irish language was unnecessary. So both our country and our native tongue had grown to wear a look of inferiority in our eyes, and when I returned from America I was at first disappointed at the apathy I saw everywhere. National feeling seemed dead.

But there were other forces at work. A few noble men were quietly planting the seeds which were soon to bring forth the fruit of a great national awakening.

Arthur Griffith in his paper, *The United Irishman*, was undermining the look-to-Westminster policy of the Parliamentary Party. He preached *Sinn Féin* (we must rely on ourselves), and was quietly carrying on and extending the work of Thomas Davis. Tom Clarke had come out of penal servitude with the Fenian tradition and was handing it on to young Seán MacDermott, who was in turn to pass it on to Michael Collins. And the Gaelic League, with its Irish classes and *ceilidhí* was breaking down the slave mind in every young man and woman who joined its ranks.

It was in the year 1900 that I became a member of the St. Lawrence O'Toole branch of the Gaelic League and began the study of my native language. The teacher and moving spirit of my branch was Patrick Merriman, M.A., who is now President of University College, Cork. He was a splendid teacher, and a charming personality. To teach his pupils was a work of love for him and, needless to say, he gave his services free, receiving no remuneration of any kind.

While I was a member of this branch I met a man who was afterwards to earn a world-wide literary reputation. He was Seán O'Casey, the dramatist. We were both working-men, and we became very friendly. I was impressed by his cleverness, and I admired his proud and independent spirit. On one occasion he lost his employment as a railway-worker in the neighbourhood, and was out of work for some time. I met him one day in the office of *Irish Freedom*, 5 Findlater Place, where he often looked in to have a chat with Seán MacDermott. I noticed that his boots were broken and letting in the wet, and, putting my hand in my pocket, I offered to lend him a pound saying he could pay me back again when he got a job. But he refused to accept the loan though I pressed him hard. He excused himself, saying that he could not contract a debt which he had no certainty of being able to repay.

I stayed on in the St. Lawrence Branch until I had learned the five books of O'Growney. I then joined the Keating Branch in Frederick Street. Cathal Brugha, afterwards Minister of Defence in the Revolutionary Government, and killed in O'Connell Street in the Civil War, was President, and here I became acquainted with a very fine set of men, nearly all of whom played splendid parts afterwards in the fight. There was Seán MacDermott, who signed the Republican proclamation and was executed after the surrender, Fionán Lynch, now Minister of Fisheries, Gearóid O'Sullivan, who became one of Michael Collins's leading men, Paddy O'Keeffe, Diarmuid O'Hegarty, Piaras Beaslai, Michael Foley, Michael Lynch, Cathal Power (now a Judge), and Con Collins. The Keating Branch came afterwards to earn a great reputation as a nursery of patriots.

CHAPTER II
I Join The Irish Republican Brotherhood

It was about this time that Arthur Griffith began to write in the *United Irishman*. I read the paper every week, and his fine, restrained, powerful writing made a great impression on me. The absence of any sentimentality, or keening for the woes of *Cáitlin na Houlihan*, gave me a new light. His message was of another kind. He would not have anything to do with poetic brooding over our sorrows. He urged us to wake up, and realize our moral strength. We could be free in Ireland and make it what we wished, *if we had the will*. That was his message.

His clear ideas and forceful words were very stimulating, and I learned to look at Ireland in a new way, gathering strength and hope from his teaching.

The Gaelic League and the Gaelic Athletic Association were the two chief sources from which the Irish Republican Brotherhood recruited its members. In proposing a man for the Brotherhood, it would be a very strong point in his favour if he was a member of the Gaelic League; and if he did not belong to the League, the next best thing to recommend him was to be able to say that he was an enthusiastic player or supporter of Hurling or Gaelic Football. If a man belonged to either of these organizations you might be fairly sure that he was possessed of certain qualities—perseverance, sincerity, honesty of purpose, and moral courage—all of them invaluable in an IRB man. When I joined the Brotherhood it gave me great delight to find these qualities in the men who became my comrades.

It was at Bodenstown in 1909, during the annual pilgrimage to the grave of Wolfe Tone, that I first became aware that the Fenian organization was still in existence.

The ceremony was over, and we were quietly resting, lying on the bank of the canal near the Railway Station at Sallins, when one of the leading men who had been in charge of the arrangements for the pilgrimage got into conversation with me. He began cautiously. He first talked about America, and spoke of the way the Fenian faith had been kept alive there by the Clan na Gael. Observing that I drank in eagerly all that he was saying, and was responsive to his words, he told me that for some time my activities in the Gaelic League had been watched by Tom Clarke and Seán MacDermott, and that he had been instructed to approach me. The old Fenian Organization had been re-established, he said. It was called the Irish Republican Brotherhood, known as the IRB, its true title being concealed under the name of Freedom Clubs, as the various circles were called. If I decided to join, he had authority

35

to enrol me as a member.

I replied that I was delighted to hear such good tidings, and would be proud to become a member, and I was there and then sworn in as a Fenian. I was told the day and the hour of the next meeting, and the name of the meeting place.

What a delightful surprise there was awaiting me at that first meeting! On entering the room, (having been closely scrutinized, as was each new comer in turn), I found myself in the midst of my closest friends of everyday life— men who belonged to the Gaelic League and other kindred organizations. I looked at them, and they looked at me, and we shook hands with warm grips, feeling a new sympathy of comradeship and affection.

Our Club was known as the Bartholomew Teeling Literary Debating Society. Each meeting-night there was laid upon the table a paper written on some historical or other harmless subject. We had to preserve it carefully so as to be able to put it out each week, because, had it got lost, another would have had to be written, to the great exhaustion of the brethren.

We were never raided, however, and we congratulated ourselves that our movements were unobserved, or rather that the real nature of them was undiscovered. But it was not so. When I was later a prisoner in Richmond Barracks awaiting court martial after the Rising, Detective Sergeant Smith (who was afterwards shot) pointed me out as a close friend of Tom Clarke and Seán MacDermott, and one who *"had never missed a monthly meeting of the IRB"*.

The business transacted at our meetings consisted in calling the roll, handing in subscriptions for the purchase of arms, proposing new men for the Brotherhood, and scrutinizing the names which were put forward as those of likely recruits for our own, or other circles. Before a man was admitted to the IRB, and the circle to which he was to belong, his name had to pass before and be approved by the members of every other circle. This was a necessary precaution. A circle was composed of ten or more members.

Arms were purchased, but in those early days not in any large quantities. We were drilled in a hall in Parnell Square. Broom handles were used for rifles, but this practice was discontinued with the organization of the Volunteers.

In my circle of the IRB there were some grand men. I will only mention a few of them here—Eamonn Ceannt, who was executed after the Rising, and The O'Rahilly, who was killed during its progress. We had also Bulmer Hobson, afterwards one of the Executive Council of the Volunteers, Richard Mulcahy, who became Chief of Staff of the Army which fought the Black and Tans, and is now Minister for Local Government in the Free State Parliament,

Eamon Duggan, afterwards one of the Signatories of the Treaty, Cathal Brugha, Piaras Beaslai, Con Collins, and Paddy O'Keeffe whom I have mentioned already as comrades of mine in the Keating Branch of the Gaelic League.

I look back upon my friendship with Tom Clarke and Seán MacDermott as among the proudest possessions of my life. There was only one other whose memory is beside theirs in my heart—a yet more shining light for me—but of him I will speak later. It is with wonderful gratitude I remember that Tom Clarke numbered me amongst his most intimate friends. I have in safe and honoured keeping a letter written to me by Mrs. Clarke thanking me in terms of eternal friendship for a service I was able to render them when they purchased their house in Richmond Road.

Tom Clarke was the connecting link between Fenianism and what came to be called Sinn Féin. In his person was kept alive the tradition of the IRB. He had been enrolled when the Brotherhood was founded by James Stephens and O'Donovan Rossa, and he survived to administer the oath to Pádraig Pearse, Seán MacDermott, and the men of '16.

His spirit was undimmed after sixteen years' penal servitude in an English prison. He came out unrepentant, and from the little tobacco shop in Parnell Street, where he established himself, and was able to earn a modest living, he became a radiating influence. The shop became the house of call of all the sincere Gaels, who, inspired by his example, were waiting for the opportunity to serve Ireland as he had done, and to make the same sacrifice.

The story of his prison life was appearing in the pages of *Irish Freedom*. Seán MacDermott was manager of the paper. Afterwards when I was arrested and a prisoner in Kilmainham Jail, uncertain what my fate was to be, I recalled Tom Clarke's story, and the memory of his greater sufferings and unbroken spirit spurred me to emulate, so far as I could, the example of his glorious courage. While I was thinking of him, the English had already shot him, and were burying his body in quicklime in the barrack yard.

CHAPTER III

I meet Seán MacDermott

When I met Seán MacDermott at a friend's house one Sunday evening in 1908 I was immediately captivated by his charming, lovable personality.

Of all the fine men who were working for Ireland in those dark, unpromising days, he was the most active. Nothing could dishearten him. He went all over the country inspiring young men everywhere with his own joyous faith. He was responsible for hundreds of recruits. When King George came to Ireland after his coronation, meetings of protest organized by him were held outside the Bank of Ireland. The Union Jack was burned, and a streamer was hung across the foot of Grafton Street, painted in large letters, with the words: *"Thou art not conquered yet, Dear Land"*.

Under the strain of all the labour he took upon himself, and his journeys, a great part on a bicycle through the country in all weathers, he was attacked by neuritis, and his health completely broke down. He suffered from severe pain in the back which no drugs could alleviate. After six months in the Mater Hospital, he came out of it on two crutches, on Christmas Eve, and came to my house in Brendan Road where he spent six weeks, trying to recover his health. He then went to Limerick to visit John Daly, another old Fenian, who had spent fourteen years in penal servitude. It was a niece of John Daly's who had become the wife of Tom Clarke.

Seán had a most fascinating way with him. He was of a gay, lively disposition, full of the spirit of the Gael. With his high spirits and charming manner he did more than anyone else in those early years to attract clever, adventurous young men into the movement. His inspiration was not merely for the moment. It lasted. The young men who fought with him in '16, who manned the barricades in the streets of Dublin where the fighting was hottest—in the King Street area and at Ashbourne—were, many of them, the same young men who afterwards fought so valiantly with Michael Collins through the horrors of the Black and Tan War.

Seán MacDermott's paper, *Irish Freedom,* was issued monthly. It rang with a fine fighting spirit and we all read it eagerly. We passed it round to other young men whom we wished to inflame with our own fervour. It was published from 5 Findlater's Place, where Seán had his Office, so that the Office became a rendezvous of the fighting Gaels. On the first of each month it was crowded. On that day the paper came back from the printer, and we all helped in the work of getting it issued. Seán had no staff; doing nearly all the writing and editing himself, so he needed help in getting the paper out. Some would be busy addressing wrappers, others in folding, and others again in sticking on the stamps. When a pile was complete, someone would rush out and put them in the letter-box round the corner. We loved those evenings. We were all merry, chatting, laughing and talking of the time we would be fighting the English. We were happy, too, because we were helping Seán.

Findlater Place has since been pulled down to make room for the new wide street which now leads from Gloucester Street to O'Connell Street. It has not yet been named, and I would like to see this new thoroughfare called after Seán MacDermott, in memory of the great work he did for Ireland on that spot. Not long ago I was standing with Gearóid O'Sullivan upon the site of the old office, and we recalled the wonderful days spent there, and the historic associations it now bears with the memory of Seán MacDermott and Tom Clarke.

Later the office of *Irish Freedom* was transferred to 12 D'Olier Street, and Seán carried on his work there up to Easter Week, working side by side with Arthur Griffith who had an office in the same building.

Early in 1915, Seán O'Hegarty, a Volunteer, was ordered to leave Cork on account of his anti-recruiting activities there. He was traced to Enniscorthy where he had taken up his residence with another active and enthusiastic Volunteer, Larry de Lacy. The house was raided and explosives found. Larry escaped, and got away to America, but Seán O'Hegarty was captured and was brought up to Dublin for trial.

Seán MacDermott, determined to get O'Hegarty off if possible, sent Seán McGarry to Glenaulin to ask Tim Healy, KC, if he would undertake his defence.

Mr. Healy at once agreed, while, looking very straight at Seán McGarry, he said: *"In my opinion you boys are Fenians"*.

McGarry made no reply, and Mr. Healy then added: *"Your silence gives consent. Never mind the hundred guineas"* (the fee to which he was entitled).

He was as good as his word, and gave his service free to the *"Fenians"*. Cathal Power was the Junior Counsel. The case attracted great attention and lasted for several days. It was thought that Seán O'Hegarty would be allowed out on bail if a substantial sum was forthcoming, and Seán MacDermott asked me to attend at Court if I were good for a thousand pounds. I agreed, and, on the advice of Cathal Power, I appeared with proof of my solvency for that amount.

Bail was refused, however, but when the case went before the jury, Seán was acquitted.

A little later Seán MacDermott himself, with Seán Milroy, was put on trial for anti-recruiting speeches. They were both found guilty and were sent to prison for two months. Seán was serving this sentence when the funeral of O'Donovan Rossa took place.

Long afterwards, Michael Collins remembered the generous action of Tim Healy in the Seán O'Hegarty case, and in another similar one, when the question of the Governor Generalship of the Free State came to be considered.

Very often Seán MacDermott and Michael Collins are side by side in my thoughts. They stand out clearly as the two most able, energetic, and courageous young men I knew, and I was acquainted with all the leading men in the movement during those years. There was a quality in both of them which drew around them the young, the gay, the brave and the adventurous. Each had personal magnetism. Each had youth, high spirits, a sense of humour and the convivial habit of the Gael. Each was gifted with just those qualities and the temperament which were needed to carry to success the work which each had to do. For his time, just such a man as Seán MacDermott was wanted, with his strong faith, yet gentle cheerfulness, to inspire young men to be prepared to leave their safe and peaceful occupations for rough and possibly dangerous work. And just such a man as Michael Collins was needed for the harder and tougher task which came to him as an inheritance out of the situation which was created by the work and sacrifice of Seán—to lead the same men into yet more daring and desperate activities, from which their chance of personal escape was small, and to toughen them for the work by the example of his own powerful and indomitable character. With all his gaiety in hours of conviviality, at other times Michael Collins had an abruptness and sternness of demeanour which was absent in Seán. Whether the hard task he set himself, and the hunted life he led, gave rise to that sternness, or whether it was always latent in his character, I do not know; but I know that it gave him a dominating influence, enabling him to carry his comrades through terrible enterprises without which what he and they did for Ireland could not have been done.

CHAPTER IV

Comrades In Arms

Another fine man of those days, though little known outside ourselves, was Hugh Houlihan. He was about forty-four years of age, and full of courage and energy. He carried on a furniture business on Usher's quay.

When King George came to Ireland after his coronation we had made a pilgrimage to Bodenstown. The procession was enormous, and we were marshalled by Hugh, an ardent and fearless Gael to whose memory I would like to pay a tribute. We marched from the station of Sallins to the grave of Wolfe Tone. An oration, breathing the true Fenian spirit, was delivered, and it was followed by patriotic songs and recitations in which we all took part.

On our return to Dublin in the evening we marched four deep from Kingsbridge along the South Quays. We had several skirmishes with the crowd on the way. Those who attacked us were mainly ex-British soldiers and loyalists, among whom were a number of women; but they got more than they bargained for. Led by Hugh Houlihan, we counter-attacked with immediate effect, and armed only with our fists, we had the pleasure of seeing the friends of England running into the first laneway they met, or scurrying down every back-alley in which they could find a refuge from our onslaught.

After that we were molested no further, and we finished our march in unbroken ranks.

Hugh's unexpected death in 1910 caused deep sorrow in the ranks of the Gaels, he was so great a favourite. He was a man of much promise, and held in the highest esteem by those who were in the inner Fenian circle of that time. Thinking of him, I am often regretting that his name was so little known, and his work for Ireland in the dark days now hardly remembered. In the strenuous years that came afterwards, with the loss of so many of our great men after Easter Week, and in the struggle which followed, many a brave man and his brave deeds were forgotten.

But Hugh lived on in his nephews, who took part in the Easter Week Rising six years afterwards. One of them, Garry Houlihan, I knew very well later on. He was a fellow-prisoner with me in the North Camp, Frongoch, and took a prominent part in our entertainments there. His recitations of patriotic ballads were full of the fighting spirit which had helped to make Easter Week possible and inspired the success of the later years.

In the early days of the Sinn Féin movement I went regularly to hear the lectures and papers read at 6 Harcourt Street. Arthur Griffith usually spoke and Alderman Tom Kelly presided. Tom Kelly, "Honest Tom" as he was justly named, was a good speaker, with a wonderful sense of humour. He was a thorough Dublin man. He knew the inner history of nearly every house in the City, and was a delightful companion on a ramble. He was splendid on the platform, and a great favourite with a Dublin audience. He knew better than anyone how to talk to the people of Dublin. He was a prisoner after the Rising, and occupied the room beside me in Richmond Barracks.

Major John MacBride lectured several times at 6 Harcourt Street. He was another good speaker, and fearless in expressing his ideas. Speaking one night of his experiences in the Boer War he described how he had seen British soldiers running away from Boer snipers and refusing to press forward an attack. *"I have seen them running away in South Africa"*, he said, *"and I live in hope of taking part in a fight in Ireland and of seeing them do the same"*. He was executed after the Rising. He died with wonderful courage and coolness. He refused to be blindfolded. *"I have been looking down the barrels of rifles all my life"*, he said.

CHAPTER V
Formation Of The Volunteers

When, in 1913, Sir Edward Carson started to arm his followers in North East Ulster to resist the putting into force of the Home Rule Act, Tom Clarke was the first man to see the opportunity which his action gave us. *"If the Orangemen can arm themselves against England"*, he argued, *"we can come into the open against England too. However different our reasons and motives they will have to adopt the same attitude to both"*.

On the suggestion of Clarke and Seán MacDermott, a big meeting was held in the Rotunda Rink, the largest hall in Dublin, capable of holding about 6,000. Half the people could not get into the Hall, and an overflow meeting was held afterwards in the street. The crowd was so enormous that the traffic was stopped, and the tram service had to come to a standstill while the meeting lasted.

All the young men were eager to be enrolled in the New Volunteer army which was to be recruited, ostensibly, in support of the Home Rule Act against the threats of Sir Edward Carson, but to the men of the IRB was to be the means by which young Irishmen could be drilled and disciplined for the carrying out of the old Fenian policy.

It was thought best that Clarke and MacDermott should not appear on the platform. Tom Clarke's name was enough to arouse suspicion, and Seán was already a marked man. Agents of the Castle had begun to hang round the little shop in Parnell Street, and due notice was taken of the men who frequented it.

So Eoin MacNeill and Larry Kettle were the principal speakers. They appealed to the men of Ireland to take up the challenge flung down in Belfast, and to protect the rights of the Irish people regardless of politics or religion. A rousing speech was also made at the overflow meeting by Bulmer Hobson whom I have already mentioned as a member (later) of the Executive Council of the Volunteers.

The splendid send-off in Dublin made recruiting in the country comparatively easy. Young men everywhere hurried to be enrolled into the ranks, and were drilled by ex-soldiers who had seen service in the British Army.

The O'Rahilly was a very active worker in getting Volunteers enrolled all over the country. Motor-cars in those days were few, and those who could afford them were not on our side. The O'Rahilly happened to own one, and he was continually on the road with it, unsparing of himself. He was also a

43

most generous subscriber to the funds.

I had of course been enrolled a Volunteer, and on the night I joined de Valera was a new recruit also.

He and I were put into the same company, and we formed fours together. We both lived in Donnybrook, and as our district was providing plenty of Volunteers a new company was soon formed of which de Valera was made a Lieutenant. He rose rapidly, and before long he was Commandant of the 3rd Battalion which was recruited from the whole of the Pembroke area of which Donnybrook formed a part.

At an Officers' Council Meeting a proposal was made by de Valera that as firearms were so difficult to obtain and as ten-foot pikes had played so large a part in the famous battle of Vinegar Hill in 1798, a supply should be procured and distributed among the Dublin Volunteers in readiness for the next fight with the English. The idea did not commend itself to the other officers present and no action was taken. But he brought up the matter again at the next meeting, and he spoke so strongly on the merits of the pike, that to please him, and fearing he might be piqued if his proposal were turned down, it was agreed to let him have his way.

Michael Staines, who was quartermaster of the Dublin Brigade, came to me: *"I am going to give you a queer order, Batt"*, he said, smiling, *"I want you to get me a gross of ten-foot ash handles for croppy pikes. Go to Gleeson & O'Deas, where they know you; they won't be suspicious, or ask you any awkward questions"*.

Gleeson & O'Deas were, however, surprised at my order.

> *"Of course we don't stock such things, Mr. O'Connor. We shall have to get them specially made and that will take a week or two. Is it for anything special you want them?"*

I mumbled something about a fence for a garden.

We had to get the pike-heads made specially, too. We got a blacksmith to forge them.

In due course, the Volunteers appeared in the streets of Dublin with their croppy pikes. But, alas! we are not the men our forefathers were. I fear we have neither their strength nor their agility. We found our weapons most cumbersome and unwieldy, and the sweat was soon pouring down our faces, and when we received the order *"About, turn!"* Well! Picture us trying to obey, each man with a ten-foot pike over his shoulder!

The bystanders fully appreciated our manoeuvres that day.

"Musha! look at the men of '98", we heard on all sides, and other comments having all the richness of expression peculiar to a Dublin mob.

That was the first and last time we paraded with our pikes.

CHAPTER VI

Volunteer Activities

I remained an active Volunteer, taking part in all the route marches and military manoeuvres. These were held usually in the Dublin mountains, so often in the past and to be in the future the 'battleground' and refuge of Dublin patriots. On one occasion we had a display at Swords on the north side of the City.

No notice was taken of our activities, or at least no steps were taken to interfere with them by the Castle people. We were pooh-poohed at first by both the English Government and the Irish Parliamentary Party. But though our numbers were never large we were strong in personnel, and we had in our leaders men of prestige, education and character. That we were a force in the country, beyond what our numbers indicated, could not be for long overlooked by John Redmond.

So he approached our Provisional Committee and asked that twenty-five of his nominees should be included upon it. He threatened, if we refused, that he would call on his supporters in the Volunteers to withdraw and form an organization of their own. As he had still a large following in the country, especially among the older people who could bring pressure to bear upon the young, and as it was necessary for us to avoid a split if possible, we gave him the representation he asked for.

But with the outbreak of the European War any hope of co-operation with the Redmondites came to an end. Our outlook was the direct opposite of theirs. Redmond's idea was that Irishmen should fight for England in France to get the English, out of gratitude, to give us the Home Rule Act which they had held up at the bidding of the Orangemen. Our idea was, in accordance with the tradition of the past, to make *"England's difficulty, Ireland's opportunity"*, and to fight against England at home.

To Tom Clarke and Seán MacDermott, representing the Fenians, to James Connolly of the Citizen Army, and to Arthur Griffith of Sinn Féin, the European War meant another chance for Ireland to renew the old struggle. To John Redmond and his Party it was a fresh opportunity to show faith in the English Government. In the British House of Commons he pledged the unconditional support of the Irish people to England's cause, and when he came to Ireland he got up on recruiting platforms and appealed to young Irishmen to go out and help England on the battlefield of France.

He went further. Without consulting their leaders, he pledged the support of the Volunteers to defend Ireland for the English against a German invasion. Arthur Griffith writing in *Sinn Féin* said:

"If the Irish Volunteers are to defend Ireland they must defend it for Ireland, under Ireland's flag and under Ireland's officers. Otherwise they will only help to perpetuate the enslavement of their country".

The Provisional Committee immediately took action, and expelled Redmond's nominees. He was forsaken even by his staunchest supporter in New York, Mr. Forde, the proprietor of the *Irish World*. But the Irish leader could no longer hear the voice of Ireland. He called upon his followers throughout the country to leave the ranks and form a Volunteer organization of their own. For the moment he was obeyed. The Volunteers broke up into two sections: our own, which became the Irish Volunteers, and the seceders, who called themselves the National Volunteers. We had eighty men in our Company in Donnybrook. After the split we had only twenty, and even those dwindled to thirteen. We were refused the use of the local Hibernian Hall where we were in the habit of assembling before and after our drilling and military exercises. We were also refused the use of the drill field.

But it was a short-lived triumph for the Redmondites, the last flicker of life in a dying movement which had controlled the country for nearly half a century. We secured a large room in Beaver Row, and started recruiting all over again. Before long we began to pull up. Fresh Volunteers joined us, and, after a while, many of those who had left us began to return. The same thing happened elsewhere, and in the end we were in as strong a position as we were before the split, and morally we were stronger because our ranks had been purged of the timid and half-hearted.

In July 1915 an event occurred which revealed the growing strength of the Irish Volunteers, and the Separatist movement, and the wane of the Redmondite influence.

News came to Ireland of the death in New York of the veteran Fenian, O'Donovan Rossa, and arrangements were made to bring home his body for burial in the Patriot's Plot in Glasnevin.

No Irishman had ever stood more strongly for the full programme of Irish Independence, or had made a more defiant resistance to English Rule, than O'Donovan Rossa. Everyone in Ireland knew by heart the story of his six years' awful sufferings in penal servitude in England, and his proud unrepentance through every effort to break his spirit.

To every Irishman and Irishwoman, therefore, his death meant a stirring of the memories of the past. It turned their minds back to the days when a small band of Fenians had stood up to the might of England; and we, who had accepted the Fenian tradition, determined to make the funeral of Rossa not only an occasion worthy of the last honours we could render to him, but to use it to remind the people of the cause to which he had devoted his life.

Thirteen Committees were formed to organize every branch of the funeral arrangements, with the Headquarters General Staff of the Irish Volunteers as a kind of Executive Council over all. I was a member of the Contingencies Committee. Elaborate as was the programme, and vast as were the crowds who attended, the obsequies were carried out in perfect order and without a hitch.

Rossa's body, as soon as it arrived in Dublin, was taken to the Pro-Cathedral, Malboro' Street. Requiem Mass was solemnized next morning in which clergymen from all parts of Ireland took part. The remains were then borne to the City Hall where they lay in state for four days. An armed guard composed of soldiers of the Irish Volunteers and the Citizen Army stood around the coffin.

Outside, the crowd waiting to enter to pay the last respects to the dead was regulated by the soldiers of both these armies, and the youths of Fianna Eireann (Irish Scouts). Of that vast crowd, each one of which waited his turn for hours to catch a glimpse of the dead face of Rossa beneath the glass lid of the coffin, it is impossible to give a picture. Never have I seen such a sight before nor since.

Special trains were run from all parts of the country. Contingents came over from England and Scotland. Almost every public body, and every organization, religious, military, political, and commercial, was represented at the funeral. A thousand members of the Women's organization, Cumann na mban, walked in the procession. Most wonderful, most moving of all was the sight of our own Irish soldiers in their green uniforms, their rifles on their shoulders, marching openly in military formation through the streets. Never shall I forget how my heart swelled with pride to see them, and with the glory of being one of them.

The procession took an hour and a half to pass any one spot, and, when the vanguard reached the cemetery, there were upwards of twenty thousand people waiting for admission.

In the City Hall an impassioned and stirring oration, full of the defiant spirit of Rossa, had been delivered by the Rev. Michael O'Flanagan, and, at the graveside, the panegyric of Pádraig Pearse will never be forgotten by those who heard it.

He had no notes. He spoke very quietly, almost gently. I was standing near him. He did not lift his eyes, but all the time kept gazing into the grave. His words though spoken so softly could be heard plainly. They seemed to come straight from his noble, sincere heart, as if, in that moment, he foresaw the future, and the sacrifice of his young life for Ireland which he was so soon to make. I was moved, uplifted, listening to that soft voice breathing a holy fervour, so that I wished for the moment to come at once, without any more delay, when I could suffer and, if necessary, die for my country. All listening to him felt the same, and many afterwards died bravely, upborne by the courage and love which came into their hearts by the grave of O'Donovan Rossa.

I would like to write down here every word of that noble oration, but it is well known, and I will repeat only a few sentences:

"I may be taken as speaking on behalf of a new generation that has been rebaptized in the Fenian faith, and that has accepted the responsibility of carrying out the Fenian Programme. I propose to you, then, that here by the grave of this unrepentant Fenian we renew our baptismal vows; that here by the grave of this unconquered and unconquerable man, we ask of God, each one for himself, such unshakable purpose, such high and gallant courage, such unbreakable strength of soul as belonged to O'Donovan Rossa."

CHAPTER VII
Preparing For The Rising

The spirit aroused at the funeral of Rossa expressed itself in the growing strength of the Volunteers, and the other military organizations, as it greatly hampered those who were looking for recruits for the British armies. Very few of the genuine Gaels, indeed, joined up at any time, but after the day of the funeral, there was a noticeable falling off.

It had now become plain to me that the work of Rossa and the Fenians was to be carried a stage further, and that another Irish generation was about to renew the old struggle with England.

This thought became a conviction when I took part in the St. Patrick's Day parade in the following March. A review was to be held in College Green, and we decided that we would make it a memorable one. The men marched with rifles and fixed bayonets, and lined the whole of the large open space in front of the Bank of Ireland, Trinity College, and the south side of Dame Street.

The review lasted for several hours, and while it was taking place British Officers in motor-cars were refused a passage through the thoroughfare. They ordered the Dublin Metropolitan Police to clear a passage for them, but the police, knowing they could not do so, persuaded them to turn back and take another route. Some of the officers got out of their cars and looked on. They could not but be impressed by the discipline and efficiency of the Volunteers, as they obeyed the words of command, and one of them was heard to say: *"If these fellows are allowed to go on like this, there will be trouble".*

I now thought well to consider what would happen to my wife and children in the event of a Rising, and my being involved in it. So I called to see a solicitor, who was a brother Volunteer, Séamus O'Connor, now Clerk of the Peace, and Registration Officer for Co. Dublin. I asked for legal advice as to whether I could safeguard my property by assigning it to another. He told me that the transference would have had to be six months in being to be effective, and that the stamp duty would cost eighty pounds. He also gave me his opinion that even if I were convicted of *"treason"*, or killed fighting against them, the British would not be likely to confiscate my property.

I came away satisfied and gave the matter no further thought.

CHAPTER VIII

The Rising

I was not on the Headquarters Staff of the Volunteers, and the date fixed for the Rising was kept a dead secret from the rank and file. Our duty was to obey orders, and to ask no questions.

On the Thursday before Easter week, I received a visit from Con Collins. He was in my circle of the IRB and was lodging in the same house as Seán MacDermott. He said he had been sent to tell me to go down to Kerry, and await the instructions I should receive there. I took this order as coming from Seán, and I packed hastily and left Dublin the same day. I went straight to my old home in Brosna where my mother was still living.

As soon as I reached Kerry I heard of the arrest of Sir Roger Casement, on the Kerry peninsula. He had come over in a German submarine to tell the leaders that he had not been able to get the men and arms he had hoped to bring over for the Rising. He knew well the risk he was taking, but he believed that the news of his failure was most important, the success of the fight depending upon the assistance which had been promised, and he determined to bring it himself. It is well known now how he landed on Banna Strand from a collapsible boat, and how the men sent down failed to meet him. He was seen, his movements aroused suspicion, and this brave and unfortunate man was betrayed to his enemies by one of his own people who was unaware of his identity.

On Good Friday came the next development. There were rumours in Brosna that important arrests had been made in Tralee, and that among the men seized were Con Collins and Austin Stack. I began to wonder about my instructions, and what I should do, as with the arrest of Con Collins the likelihood of my being of any use in Kerry was becoming remote.

On Easter Monday the local Post Office was closed by the police, acting on instructions from Dublin. We learned that the Rising had begun, and that the General Post Office was occupied by the Volunteers.

Nearly all the people in the village were hostile.

They spoke bitterly of the leaders in Dublin as *"rebels"* and *"pro-Germans"*, and said they were *"ruining the country"*. I kept very quiet, not giving myself away, until, at last, listening to one man expressing the most mean and unpatriotic sentiments, and fretted by my own uncertain position, I lost my temper. I told him what I thought of him, and my words were repeated to the police, so that I found myself being closely watched.

I had already made up my mind to wait no longer, but to get back to Dublin where there would at least be work for me to do, and I determined to slip away out of Kerry at once.

But before I left I had the pleasure of finding two good men who were heart and soul in sympathy with the *"rebels"*. One was David Horgan, now a Peace Commissioner, and the other was Aeneas C. Guiney, now Income Tax Collector. Aeneas suspected I was down in Kerry on business. *"Look here, Batt"*, he said to me, confidentially, *"though you are keeping so quiet, I know you are not down here for nothing. I want to tell you I have a double-barrelled shot gun, and, if there is anything doing, you can count on me"*.

Strange to say, both Horgan and Guiney were afterwards supporters of the Treaty, while those in Brosna who had cursed us as pro-Germans in '16 were all strong against it because it did not go far enough and secure a Republic.

On the first day I got as far as Newcastle West. On the way I called to see some friends at Abbeyfeale, but was told by them that there was no sign of any activity in that part of the country. I next reached Limerick and saw the barricades which were being erected by the British on each side of the bridge which spans the Shannon. But again no sight of the Volunteers! The following day I got as far as Ballybrophy by train where we were all turned out. We were told that the line had to be kept clear for the trains carrying British troops to Dublin.

There was no accommodation for travellers at Ballybrophy, and I was glad to be allowed to sit all night on a chair in the kitchen of a public-house.

It was now the Saturday of Easter Week, and in the morning I was able to get a train which brought me to Lucan. Here we were again ejected. I tried to hire a car to drive me by a roundabout way to Dublin, but no matter what money I offered I could not get one. I was obliged to spend that night in Lucan, and in the morning there was nothing for it but to risk taking a tram to the City.

Before doing so I emptied my pockets and my bag and got rid of anything likely to incriminate me.

At Kingsbridge there was a military cordon across the street. I was questioned as to who I was and where I came from. I had my story ready. I was a builder's foreman, employed on a job outside the City, and was returning to my home.

I was just about to be given the necessary passport to enable me to pass into Dublin, when, as ill luck would have it, I was recognized by a well-known Dublin detective who was with the British soldiers for identifying purposes.way out of Kerry at once.

"Hold that man", he said, *"I have seen him before. I have seen him often in the company of Tom Clarke."*

"What! Who is Tom Clarke?" said the officer, puzzled.

"Why! don't you know?" said the detective, surprised at the officer's ignorance, *"he is a leader of the rebels. He signed the Republican declaration"*.

The officer was at once all excitement. *"Seize him!"* he cried: *"get a guard!"*

CHAPTER IX

Arrested

I was held a prisoner during the day in the waiting-room of the Lucan Tramways. Soldiers were on guard on the place which was being used as a clearing house for prisoners.

By the state of the room you could see that it had been well used, but at the moment there was only one other prisoner besides myself. He was a builders' labourer, he told me. He had no connection with the Rising. When he was held up and asked where he was going, he had replied: *"I am going to the Barracks".* He was employed there doing some repairs, but the word *"barracks"* had undone him.

He was very downhearted. He sat cursing his luck, cursing the British, and cursing the *"rebels"* for the trouble they were bringing on the country.

Though I cannot say I felt cheerful, thinking of my wife and children at home, yet I knew the Rising was right, just as we knew that it could not succeed as a military effort. We had once more asserted the right of our nation to armed resistance. That had been our object, and we had achieved it. Dublin had been held for a week by a handful of Volunteers. The people would be inspired again. Future generations could not say that ours alone had failed to make a gesture of defiance to England.I had a small flask in my bag. I took it out and offered a drink to my companion. I had no sooner put it to my own lips than an officer passing through the room yelled at our guard, asking him *"what the hell"* did he mean allowing drink among his prisoners. I quickly swallowed a few mouthfuls before it was taken from me.

While I had been groping for my flask in my bag, my eye had caught sight of a few bullets which I had overlooked when I had searched my possessions at the 'frontier'.

This was a most unpleasant discovery. I was bound to be searched, and if I were found with the bullets there was no hope of escape for me. My mind got working as to how I could get rid of them.

"I beg your pardon", said I, addressing the soldier in charge, *"my feet got wet walking to the City this morning. I am subject to rheumatism. Would you mind if I put on a dry pair of socks?"*

Permission granted, in taking out the socks I managed, unnoticed, to transfer the bullets to my jacket pocket.

Then I espied a chunk of bread lying on the floor under a bench on the other side of the room.

"If I may trouble you again", I said, *"I have had nothing to eat since an early breakfast, and I am faint with the hunger. I see a piece of bread over there on the floor. Would there be any objection to my having it?"*

"If you care for it, you can 'ave it", he replied, with a grin of contempt for the low habits of the Irish.

Well, while I was making a pretence of taking a bite of it, I managed to squeeze first one bullet and then the other, which I had hidden in the palm of my hand, into the soft part of the dough, and, as soon as I had done so, I made a face of disgust at the staleness of the bread, and, with a suitable exclamation, I threw it back again under the seat.

Soon after the officer in charge passed again through the room.

"What do you mean", he cried angrily, *"allowing your prisoners to spit on the floor, making it into such a filthy mess? Get them a bucket of water, and see that they wash it"*, he shouted, going out.

My companion began to protest:

"It was not us chaps that done all that spitting, most of it was here before we came".

"Come on", said I, quietly, seeing my chance, *"let us do it. What matter? It will pass the time"*.

We were led out to a tap in the yard, where we filled the buckets. We got down on our knees and set to work. Very soon I edged my way over to where my abandoned crust was lying, and I swept it into the bucket. My task finished, I carried out the slops and emptied them down the sink in the yard.

I had got rid of any direct evidence to implicate me. I breathed freely once more.

In the evening I was taken with others to Kilmainham Jail. As we were led through the streets the crowd showed no sympathy with us. Some were even hostile. Seeing me, a woman on the pavement called out to my guard not to trouble to take me a prisoner but to shoot me. Looking straight at her I shouted back: *"What have I done against you?"* But the guard ordered me to shut up, and move on.

Arrived at Kilmainham, I was put into a bare room with my fellow-prisoner, the builders' labourer.

Alone, but for this one companion with whom I could not share my feelings, I began to think of my wife and children, wondering how they would manage without me. I thought of my mother in Kerry, now an old woman. I feared she would be heartbroken thinking about me and the seriousness of my position. Next day I was to meet a fellow-prisoner who was to give me very good advice upon this matter, which was to benefit me greatly both then and afterwards.

CHAPTER X

Kilmainham Jail

On that night, my first in prison, I had a narrow escape from death.

There was no sanitary convenience in the room and, being locked in, we could not get to the lavatory outside. When it had become quite dark I began to wonder if I had perhaps overlooked some arrangement in the room for the convenience of prisoners in this respect. I was standing close to the window. I struck a match.

The moment it flared two shots were fired at the window in quick succession from outside. The glass was shattered and I was covered with the flying mortar and dust. At the report of the firing the squad turned out, and some of them rushed into the room, with arms presented, and proceeded to search me. The sentry outside had supposed that one of the prisoners was making an attack on him. My matches were taken from me and I was threatened with punishment if I was responsible for any more alarms.

The next morning I was moved into a large room where there were about thirty prisoners. Most of them were unknown to me. They had been rounded up in the general indiscriminate arresting after the surrender and many of them were soon released.

Among the prisoners in the room, there was a young lad, Matt Connolly, fifteen years old, a brother of Seán's. Seán had been killed fighting behind the parapet on the roof of the City Hall. Matt, who was on the roof with him, had crept over to his aid when Seán was hit, but so great was his fatigue after the long week of fighting without rest, that when he was captured he was found lying, fast asleep, across the dead body of his brother.

Among the majority in the room there was an air of depression. Our guard, unlocking the door and coming in from time to time to have a look at us, or to bring us a meal of weak oatmeal porridge, brought disquieting rumours. We were told that owing to the burning of Boland's bakery the loaf had risen to four shillings. One of my fellow-prisoners began to lament grievously upon hearing this news. When he had left home to take part in the Rising there was only five shillings in the house. *"Ah, what will they do at all"*, he kept repeating, wringing his hands: *"my poor little children, what will become of them?"*

It was then I heard the good counsel I have spoken of! It was given to us by an American, James Sullivan, who had been arrested on suspicion of aiding and abetting the Rising. He told us that he had been in several revolutions in South America and had been in prison there, and that he had learned a way to bear such reverses of fortune with equanimity.

"Do not let your thoughts wander outside these walls", he said. *"You cannot help your relatives and friends by thinking of them; you cannot lessen their anxiety or add to their comfort. On the other hand, by dwelling on their possible troubles you are weakening your own resolution. Men"*, he cried, *"a*

day will come when you would lose your right arm", flinging out his own, *"rather than have missed the glory of what you are suffering now"*.

His words seemed words of wisdom to me, and I practised his advice with great benefit to myself. I was disappointed to see that it did not bring the same consolation to my companions.

There was no furniture of any kind in the room which was not nearly large enough for the number of men occupying it. When we were tired walking about we sat on the floor, and were glad to have a wall to lean against.

When night came we lay down on the bare boards. There was not enough room to stretch ourselves at full length so that we lay with our bodies curved, each man resting his head on the shoulder of the man lying beside him.

Early in the morning I was awakened out of a fitful doze by the noise of a volley of rifle fire in the yard below. It was the sound of the shots which put an end to the lives of Tom Clarke, Pádraig Pearse, and Thomas MacDonagh, the first three of our leaders to be executed, but I did not know then what those ominous sounds meant.

Later in the day, looking out of the window, we caught sight of Joe Plunkett and two other prisoners in the yard. They had just been court martialled at Richmond Barracks (I learned afterwards) and had been condemned to death. While I watched them they were emptying their pockets, apparently at the bidding of their guard, throwing the contents on the ground. They had only a few cigarettes and loose matches.

I saw a priest arrive, and linking his arm in Joe Plunkett's they walked up and down for a long time talking. Grace Gifford, Joe's sweetheart, was allowed into the prison that night and was married to him a few hours before his death.

CHAPTER XI

We Hear We Are To Be Shot

That day was Wednesday. In the afternoon a military sergeant unlocked the door. I was standing by myself near it as he entered. We took very little notice of the comings and goings of our guard but this fellow began to speak to me. He told me that three of our leaders had been shot that morning at dawn. This was the first news we got of the executions.

"I am sorry for you chaps", he said, *"I am afraid the same fate is in store for you. A ton of quicklime came in this morning and they are digging a large trench outside big enough to hold a hundred"*.

As soon as he went out my companions gathered round me to know what he had been saying. I told them.

Up to that moment there had been a babel of voices in the room but now silence fell upon us all. Every man was thinking hard. Then suddenly one moved over towards the wall and fell upon his knees. We all followed suit.

We had a few prayer books amongst us and in some cases two men read out of the same book, holding it between them. I made a fervent act of contrition and then, having finished my prayers, I chanced to look over the shoulder of my companion. He was reading the Litany for the Dying!

One of the men whom I knew amongst us was Leo Rinn. He was a carpenter by trade. He had been badly wounded in the fight and was still in his uniform which was covered with bloodstains. He was not kneeling. He was sitting on the ground with his back to the wall. He was the first to break the silence:

"We have prayed long enough now", he said: *"whatever our fate is to be, we cannot avoid it. Let us cheer up and have a song"*.

He sang the first verse of *The Soldiers' Song* (which is now our National Anthem) with a clear steady voice, and by the time he reached the chorus we had caught his courage and were all ready to join in.

The door was again opened and the same Sergeant entered.

"Well, I'm blowed", he said, *"here are all you fellows going to be shot any minute, and you spend your time singing and enjoying yourselves"*.

"Why not?" said Leo Rinn. *"Irishmen can die singing as well as any other way"*.

Amongst us were some men who had had nothing to do with the Rising. They had been arrested for looting. When they had heard what the Sergeant said about the quicklime, they went deadly pale. They drew away at once by themselves into a corner as if our nearness would contaminate them. We were condemned men and they were terrified that they might share our fate. They did not pray at all but began damning and cursing us.

"Oh, you bloody rebels", they whimpered, *"you are the cause of all our*

troubles. Here we are, poor innocent men, and maybe we will be shot, and we having nothing at all to do with your bloody rebellion".

"All I got was a pair of boots", wailed one of them, *"and them too small for me!"*

But none of us was shot.

Next day we were sorted out. The 'innocent' were set free, and I was transferred to Richmond Barracks with some other prisoners to await court martial.

CHAPTER XII

A Prisoner In Richmond Barracks

The first day I was put into the gymnasium which was filled with a large crowd of prisoners. Here I found de Valera and Dr. Hayes, both of whom were most anxious to hear what I had to report from Kerry and Limerick. I was sorry I had no better news to tell them than that all was quiet in those counties.

The following day, with de Valera, I was moved into a room with thirty others and here I remained until I was transported to England about a month later.

Among my companions were Count Plunkett (the father of Joe who had been executed), Diarmuid Lynch, William O'Brien, and Thomas Foran of Liberty Hall (Irish Transport Workers' Union), Darrel Figgis, Patrick Mahon (the printer), Douglas Ffrench Mullen, Seán T. O'Kelly, a member of the Dublin Corporation, Hugh O'Hehir, the late Henry Dixon (solicitor), Joe Murray, Gerard Crofts (the singer), big John O'Mahony, Larry O'Neill (Lord Mayor of Dublin), and Jack Larkin.

I was greatly delighted to find myself among so many friends and I shook hands heartily with them all. I told them of my experiences and listened to the story of theirs. I had to hear from them the full narrative of the Rising, and as each man's part in it was separate and different, it took us all the time we were together to exchange our news.

In Richmond Barracks, as in Kilmainham, we had no beds, bedding, or furniture. The weather continued very cold and we had great difficulty in getting any sleep. We took off our boots and used them as pillows and anyone who had an overcoat was able to use it as a blanket.

We all felt great pity for the aged Count Plunkett both on account of the execution of his son, of which he had not yet heard, and because he must have felt the hardship of the place more than many of us who had had to rough it from time to time. He could not sleep at all lying on the floor and never lay down. We managed to get an empty orange box from one of the soldiers and, putting it against the wall, he sat on it throughout the night. One young man insisted on spreading his overcoat around his knees to keep him warm, and another wrapped his round the Count's shoulders.

Our dinner was served in two large buckets placed in the middle of the floor. There were no knives or forks or mugs or any utensils. In the buckets were potatoes and small pieces of meat all cooked together. We stood round the buckets trying to pull out portions of the stew with bits of sticks and biscuits. Seeing our plight, one of the soldiers brought us a few empty condensed milk tins. With the help of these to ladle out our portions, and some hard biscuits, we managed quite well.

In Richmond Barracks I found a great number of men with whom I was intimately acquainted, mainly Volunteers, all of whom had had some part in the Rising. They were soldiers prepared to take the fortunes of war and I found them cheerful and full of courage.

We formed ourselves into an organization with John O'Mahony as Commandant for the time being. Each man had his office and duties. Big John had managed to bribe one of our guard, the cook, sergeant of the officers' mess, to bring in a bottle of whisky occasionally. It was then cheap, five shillings and sixpence a bottle outside, and we paid the soldier seven shillings and sixpence for it. It was my duty as Storekeeper to keep charge of the bottle, which I kept secreted up the chimney during the day. When we could not get to sleep at night on account of the cold we would get up and walk about a bit, stamping our feet. This was often the signal for a nip of whisky to warm us. John would order me, *"Storekeeper, get your keys and unlock the safe"* and, nothing loth, I would bring forth the bottle from its hiding place.

The day before we were all separated John had only a pound note which he gave to our friend, the soldier, with instructions to bring back the change, but the fellow knew, (which we did not), that we were to be moved next day, and we never got our whisky and John never saw his money again.

One day Count Plunkett had to go to the dispensary to see the Doctor. When he gave his name he was asked, *"Are you the father of Joseph Plunkett who was shot?"* That is how he heard the news of the death of his son which he bore with great fortitude. We were heart-broken, not knowing how to show our sympathy.

To pass the time we set up a court. De Valera was charged with being a Pretender to the throne of Dalkey Island. Count Plunkett was appointed Judge, and counsel for the accused and for the prosecution were William O'Brien, Pat Mahon, Lord Mayor O'Neill, and J.J. Reynolds. A jury was empanelled after a lot of objections from counsel on both sides. But we proceeded no further. De Valera's court martial was fixed for the next day. *"Look here, I think we won't go on with this"*, he said, *"it is getting on my nerves"*. We suddenly realized that we were rehearsing what was going to be for him a very serious drama on the morrow.

The next morning the fellows were all gathered around him. He was waiting for his summons and each of his friends was asking him for a keepsake. He gave away everything he had in his pockets including his fountain pen. Yet there were not enough mementoes to go round and they began to cut off the buttons from his tunic. As all the officers commanding during the Rising had been shot, his fate seemed certain. He was very brave, and outwardly calm. I was the last man to shake hands with him.

"Good-bye, Batt", he said, *"we may not meet again. You know I am expecting—that!"* imitating with his hand the firing of a gun.

CHAPTER XIII

Deported

No one helped more to make us forget our situation than Gerard Crofts. He sang to us continually and listening to him we forgot our troubles. Our favourite song was *Cockles And Mussels, Alive, Alive Oh*. We never tired hearing it and he gave it with great animation. He sang four or five songs for us on the morning of his court martial.

While I was a prisoner in Richmond Barracks my wife was allowed to visit me. We looked at each other across a barbed wire fence and it was great joy to me to see her in such courage and good spirits as it was to her to find me well and cheerful.

While we were looking at each other in such strange circumstances a thought occurred to me. *"Bring Brendan with you the next time you come"*, I said to her. He was our little son, aged then about four years. It had come to my mind, that, seeing his father a prisoner, the picture of his father behind that barbed wire fence would be printed indelibly on his memory. *"He will be sure then to grow up a good Irishman"*, I thought.

Before I was deported she was allowed into the Barrack Square to take over what money I had upon me when I was searched after my arrest Lieutenant Robert Barton was the military officer who had charge of the prisoners' effects. It was through coming in contact with the prisoners at this time that he became converted to our Cause. He brought my wife to the room where I was a prisoner, so that he could hand my money to her in my presence for which I signed a receipt. Then he saw her back to the gate. His manner was full of kindness and courtesy, in marked contrast to the abrupt and often offensive behaviour of the other British officers, and my wife never forgot him.

A few years afterwards she had an opportunity of showing her appreciation. When Mr. Barton was himself a prisoner in 1919, and his rescue from Mountjoy was decided upon, it was arranged that he should come to my house in Brendan Road. When he arrived my wife and he immediately recognized each other. We were delighted to have him as our guest and she could never do enough for him while he was with us.

The sorting out of the prisoners was going on all the time I was in Richmond Barracks. They were brought out in batches each day into the square. They were lined up, scrutinized by the Dublin detectives, and sent for court martial, or shipped at once to England for internment.

Alderman Tom Kelly, Paddy O'Keeffe, and Gearóid O'Sullivan (afterwards Adjutant-General of the Free State Army) were in the next room to the one I occupied.

Paddy O'Keeffe had been a civil servant employed in the Post Office. It became known that he was an active Volunteer and he was warned by the postal authorities that he must not have anything to do with such an organization. So his OC had told him to keep quiet and not to turn out on parade.

When the Rising started on Easter Monday he was at home. All day he sat waiting, listening to the noise of the guns, waiting for the dark. As soon as evening fell he took his rifle, bandolier and ammunition, and said good-bye to his wife. She knew of his intention and agreed with it. Mrs. O'Keeffe was a very brave Irishwoman sharing all her husband's risks. She was one of our best helpers, clever and fearless, during the greater dangers of subsequent years.

By back streets, Paddy had made his way to the GPO and reported himself to his superior officer. He fought in the O'Connell Street area all through the Rising and had a very narrow escape from death. The English occupied a building at the angle of D'Olier Street and Westmoreland Street, and they raked the whole of O'Connell Street with continual machine gun fire while Paddy lay flat in the street for over an hour, the bullets flying round him.

He was arrested after the surrender.

In Richmond Barracks, Seán MacDermott was in another room on the same corridor. One day, looking out of the window, we saw Seán in the Square. To our relief we saw him among the batch who were to be marched to the boat for internment in England. But our joy was short-lived. The detectives appeared. He was picked out and put among those for court martial. He was shot a few days afterwards.

During the first days in Richmond Barracks the military officers were rather hostile. On the least provocation they would become violent in their language, threatening us with all kinds of punishment. A very dogged officer was Major Orr. He was not only hard upon the prisoners but on his own men as well.

Every morning six prisoners were told off to attend to the sanitary arrangements. These were on the usual camp model and were situated in the Barrack yard, behind a canvas awning. The conveniences for the English soldiers were the same and, though separate, were alongside those we used. It was one of our duties to clean out the latrines used by us and this was done by the fatigue party appointed for the day.

On the fifth morning it was the turn of a party led by Gearóid O'Sullivan. When they had done the job, they received an order to clean the latrines used by the English soldiers. Gearóid at once refused. He said he was prepared to take his turn in attending to the requirements of his comrades, but that nothing would induce him to do so for the English soldiers.

The Sergeant of the guard hurried off to report the matter to Major Orr. The Major arrived immediately in a towering rage. O'Sullivan repeated his refusal. Saying he would give him two minutes to obey, the Major walked back five paces and, drawing his revolver, he took his watch in his other hand.

This scene took place in the Barrack yard, and from the window of the room in which we were imprisoned we watched all that was passing below.

We could see the Major's lips moving, and the resolute expression and unflinching attitude of Gearóid. I have thought the world of him since that day.

When the two minutes were up Major Orr repeated his challenge, but already he knew he was beaten, and calling some of his men to arrest them, he ordered O'Sullivan and the five men with him to be taken to solitary confinement, preparatory to being court martialled for refusing to obey a military order.

The trial was held the next day. The military authorities decided that it was not the duty of the prisoners to clean the latrines of the soldiers and O'Sullivan and the other men were released. His courageous act was the means of freeing the rest of us from what would have been an extremely unpleasant addition to our already not-over-pleasant labours.

My own turn had already come. Six hundred of us were lined up one morning on the order of the the military officer in charge. We were looked over by the inspector, one by one. Just when I thought I had not been recognized I was told to stand out. Diarmuid Lynch was a companion in misfortune with me. We were both ordered for court martial and sent back to our room. Diarmuid was sentenced to be shot. But he was an American citizen and that fact saved his life. His sentence was commuted to twenty years' penal servitude.

Probably owing to the arrival of Mr. Asquith in Dublin, and other events which eased the situation, my own court martial, and that of many others, never came off. Anyhow, I found myself one morning one of a large batch of prisoners who were to be marched to the North Wall.

The man walking beside me was my friend, Paddy O'Keeffe. The prisoner walking on my other side was Dick Fitzgerald, the famous Captain of the Kerry football team. By some means, Paddy O'Keeffe's wife and mine had heard we were to be transported that morning. They were waiting for us and as we marched along the middle of the street, surrounded by a strong guard, they kept pace with us on the pavement.

A great crowd of people accompanied us on our march through the streets.

There was a marked change in their attitude to the prisoners. In place of the former hostility, there was nothing but friendliness shown us. Amongst the crowd were many friends and, in spite of our guard who were heavily armed, they would rush from the pavements and succeed in shaking hands with us. Sometimes we felt things being pushed into our pockets during these encounters.

When we reached Commons Street, North Wall, the crowd was allowed no further.

I took a last lingering look at my wife wondering how long it would be before I would see her face again.

CHAPTER XIV

Wandsworth Jail

From the deck of the ship we watched Ireland receding. None of us had a word to say while there was a blur left on the horizon which we could fancy was the Dublin Mountains.

But when at last there was nothing but sea around us, we turned to each other, and thinking to see what had been pushed into our pockets during our march to the quays, three of us found ourselves the happy possessors of two half bottles of whisky each. So we threw off our melancholy, and did our best to drown our sorrows and regrets.

We did not know whither we were bound, but on landing we learned that we were at Holyhead.

There was a special train waiting for the prisoners of whom there were about 500. We were in the charge of a strong military guard. Ten prisoners were put into each compartment, each with an armed soldier on guard. Our guard did not sit down at all but remained standing during the whole journey to London. Owing to air raids, the windows were heavily curtained so we got no glimpse whatever of the country we were passing through.

On leaving Richmond Barracks each of us had been provided with a tin of bully beef and hard biscuits, and we took care to consume these on our way as we had heard that we would not be allowed to bring any food with us beyond the prison gate.

Among the men in my compartment were Paddy O'Keeffe and J.J. O'Connell, the latter known amongst us as Ginger O'Connell. O'Connell was afterwards a General in the Free State Army, and it was his kidnapping by the Irregulars in 1922 which led to the attack on the Four Courts at the beginning of the Civil War.

When we reached London we were lined up on the platform of the station.

Here we aroused a good deal of curiosity. The ladies, we noticed, were more ready to draw near and stare at us than the men, and to make remarks that we could hear.

"These cannot be German prisoners", they said.

One middle-aged woman adjusted her glasses and took a searching look at John O'Mahony.

"Quite good-looking men!" she declared. *"What **can** they have done? How very sad!"*

John was a splendid looking fellow, six foot two inches high, and broad in proportion, and we chaffed him a good deal over his lady admirer.

I parted from Big John at the station, and from Joe Murray, and from many others. They were sent, some to Reading Jail, and some to Lewes.

I was one of the batch taken to Wandsworth Prison, and with me were Paddy O'Keeffe, Gearóid O'Sullivan, William Sears (afterwards a Senator), Maurice Collins, Henry Dixon, Seán T. O'Kelly, Joe Derham, and Liam O'Brien, now Professor in Galway University.

The first days in prison seemed endless in their lonely, dreary monotony. I was confined to my narrow cell for twenty-two hours out of the twenty-four. Besides my plank bed, I had only a small wooden stool.

Every time the heavy door of my cell, with its powerful spring lock, was banged upon me, my heart fell despondently. The warders wore rubber-soled shoes and their noiseless movements gave me an added sense of the eeriness of the place. Wandsworth Jail is in my memory a sinister dungeon, full of gloom and despair, in which human beings moved about in a sly, sneaking, ashamed sort of fashion.

I am of a sociable disposition. My delight in life is to meet my cronies, have a drink with them, and talk over the experiences we have shared together. In Wandsworth I looked back with longing to our days in Richmond Barracks where, while we had great sorrows to bear in the deaths of our beloved leaders and serious personal anxieties, yet I had the relief of continual social intercourse.

Sitting on my hard stool, with my back to the wall, I tried to put into practice the philosophy of my American friend, Sullivan. I did my best not to let my thoughts wander home, but I must confess that I did not always succeed very well. I think I was helped most by keeping before my mind the similar but greater sufferings which Tom Clarke had borne so bravely. *"If he could live through this for fourteen years, surely I can bear it for a little while"*, I would say to myself.

I also got strength from the thought of O'Donovan Rossa, of his brave spirit which no prison terrors could destroy. I kept before my mind, so far as I could, the honour it was for me to be a humble walker in the footsteps of those noble men.

For hours and hours I sat upon my stool. From time to time something would cause me to look up, and I would see the little shutter being drawn back which covered the spy-hole in the door of my cell. In the aperture, an eye-ball appeared and stared at me for a moment. Even the lid of the eye could not be seen. Then it would be withdrawn, and the shutter slowly and noiselessly replaced. There was no sound outside to suggest that there was a human shape attached to that uncanny eye.

My bed was the usual plank bed, raised about three inches from the floor. There was no mattress. I could not sleep on it at all at first with its unaccustomed hardness into which no part of my body could relax. My hip bones got very sore and the pain of them would keep me turning over from side to side.

But after a while I got used to it, and through sheer fatigue I would manage to sleep.

But there was another inconvenience for which there was no cure until the real midsummer weather set in. It was the cold. The bed covering was miserably scanty, and with nothing underneath me to give me any enveloping warmth. I would wake shivering after an hour or two of sleep. My feet, especially, were perished, and I would get up and stamp about the floor several times in the night, trying to bring some circulation into them. Only, the space was so narrow when the bed was let down that I could not move backwards and forwards for more than a foot or two. I jumped and hopped from one foot to another. Another good means of getting warm was to seize my stool and swing it above my head, first with one arm and then with the other. On many a night I got up three times to go through these performances after which I was able to sleep for a little.

Even in the daytime I was cold through sitting for so long. The prison books given to us to read were not very interesting. There was an arithmetic, and a book about botany, and a hymn book. I found I could not concentrate very well on the matter. In the early days, for one thing, I was always hungry. I had a steady longing for food, and kept thinking of a dish of bacon and cabbage such as I enjoyed at home. So I could not keep my mind on the page before me. The cold of my feet, too, was a continual distraction.

Also I was pestered in the daytime by the everlasting movements of the prisoner who occupied the cell directly above mine. The floors were boarded and this prisoner wore very strong boots with hobnails. He paced his cell for hours on end and I was tortured listening to him.

I tried to find out who he was and learned at last that he was a brave, hefty fellow from County Galway. I managed to get an opportunity to have a word with him and told him of my trouble. He was sympathetic. He promised he would take his exercise in future in a pair of stout homespun socks which his mother had knitted for him. I asked him why he did not sit down sometimes and read.

"I finished the arithmetic", he said, *"half an hour after I got it"*.

Our breakfast consisted of a three-inch cube of dark solid war bread and a pint of cocoa. For dinner, we had thin, colourless broth with a few shreds of meat in it, and a few potatoes, which were half cold and of inferior quality. Supper was a repetition of the morning meal.

I was sick with hunger and the craving for food, and when it came at last it was so insufficient that it seemed merely to whet my appetite. It was of no more use to me than the plate of soup with which one begins a good dinner—merely a preparation for what was to follow. But in prison nothing followed, and when I had carefully picked up and swallowed any crumbs which I had let fall I wondered how I would be able to bear my empty stomach until the next meal arrived.

I noticed a definite time-table in regard to the hunger pains from which I suffered. Immediately after eating, for about half an hour, they were very persistent; then they would ease off somewhat, and for an hour or two I was able to stop thinking continuously of my longing for food. Then, again, for the couple of hours before the next meal they would take hold of me, to my torment.

I believe if we had got no relief, and I had had to live on the prison fare for long, my idea of happiness would have become inseparable from the thought of eating. My dreams of freedom would have been largely concerned with the amount of food I would then be at liberty to consume.

Another thing which distressed me was never knowing the time of day. I could not tell whether I had still to wait one hour or only half an hour before I would again get something to eat. When the food came at last I had finished it in two or three minutes, and had to reconcile myself to the thought that it would be another five hours, all but those few minutes, before anything would be given to me again.

The long, lightsome evenings in June seemed endless, and I waited in weariness for the eight o'clock bell which was the signal to go to bed.

I took down my bed boards and unfolded the few thin strips of covering and lay down. I stared for hours vacantly at the ceiling. The window was only a small aperture fixed close to the top of the wall so that the rays of light coming in could not penetrate very far. Owing to its height, I could not see anything outside, so that I only saw the sky when I was at exercise.

But when the sun shone it threw a shadow on the opposite wall of my cell and this became my timepiece. I got to notice where it fell at four, six, and eight o'clock—the hours when the prison bell was rung; so that in between those hours, by the position of the shadow, I could make a guess at the time. When the sun failed to shine my calculations were upset.

CHAPTER XV
Some Alleviations Of Our Sufferings

After some weeks we got a concession which gave us great relief and put an end to the worst of my miseries. We were allowed to see visitors in the waiting-room near the entrance of the prison and to receive small parcels of food.

Our Irish people in London took most generous advantage of this permission. The girls showered parcels upon us. Some of them were nurses on night duty and they would give up several hours of their daytime sleep to come to Wandsworth with presents of fruit and cake.

Many of us got parcels from home too, and our kind London friends also arranged and paid for an eight-ounce white baker's bun to be sent in daily to each prisoner. I cannot describe our satisfaction. With these gifts, and the prison allowance of eight ounces of war bread, we were now getting enough nourishment for men in confinement who were doing no work.

So that, growing more accustomed to the hard bed and the long hours of solitude, my lot was more bearable.

But there were amongst us a few who never became resigned to their fate. They were for ever sighing and grumbling, longing for home, and wondering how long they would be kept prisoners. I always tried to shun a man who was continually whining. I preached the Sullivan doctrine, but to no use. It never caught hold of them and they would not even try to make an effort.

Life was getting more tolerable week by week. In time I was given a mattress and as we were now into the month of July I got hardly to mind the thinness of my bedclothes.

Every Sunday at Mass I had the pleasure of catching sight of Arthur Griffith, also of George Nicholls of Galway. These men and a few other prisoners were in a wing of the prison apart from ours and we never saw them except at Mass.

It struck me as very strange in the prison chapel that the warders sat on very high seats placed against the wall on each side. They were set above the prisoners and spent the whole time staring down at them, their eyes roving round to mark for punishment any prisoner they saw whispering or trying to speak to the man next him. They never once looked towards the priest or the altar.

Douglas Ffrench Mullen was a fellow-prisoner at Wandsworth. He was a good pianist and could also play the organ. One day he suggested to the prison chaplain that he should be allowed to play for the hymns. Permission was given and he played the following Sunday. As we stood up to pass out of the chapel in file, Douglas was still at the organ, and imagine our feelings when we suddenly heard the strains of *The Soldiers' Song*.

We were fairly taken off our feet. He played the whole of the first verse, and when he came to the chorus it was all we could do to refrain from raising our voices. For a few moments the prison vanished. We were back at home among our own. The throb of our hearts might have been heard by a sensitive ear; and I fear our emotion was noted, because, though the air was quite unknown to our jailers, Douglas was, if I remember rightly, kept away from the organ for the future.

At first, when we were taken out for exercise, we were made to march around the asphalt circles, a wider outer one, and a narrow inner one, each man at a fixed number of paces from the man in front of him. If we drew nearer we were shouted at, and if we made any attempt to talk we were punished.

But with the coming of other concessions we were also now exempted from walking in the ring. One day it was announced that we could move about as we pleased and converse together.

It is hard to describe the scene which followed. Men who had not seen each other since the days before the Rising, except at the tantalizing distance of the ring, now rushed towards each other and began to embrace and shake hands. Questions were poured out too fast for the answers. Who was killed in action? Who was executed? What happened to Liam this and Peadar that? In what area were you fighting? Was there much of the City burned? What parts of the country outside Dublin put up any fight at all?

In the beginning we were only allowed two hours in the exercise yard and on that first day the order to *"Fall in"* came all too soon. We felt we had been only talking to each other for a few minutes.

Then another grand thing happened. We got permission to receive newspapers. Alderman Alfred Byrne, who was then a member of the British Parliament, heard of this, and he came at once to see us bringing with him a big bundle of Irish daily papers. None of us who got one of them that day will ever forget his thoughtfulness. Only those who were in English prisons could understand the immense pleasure it was to us to see any kind of newspaper from home. Even to read the well-known advertisements of the Dublin shops gave us a throb of joy.

Another splendid friend was Lawrence Ginnell, MP. He came regularly to see the prisoners, and into the capacious pockets of the black frock coat he invariably wore we would slyly push the letters we did not wish to be read by the censors. He pretended not to notice what we were doing, but the letters always reached their destinations.

During the month of July we heard that we were to be transferred to an Internment camp in Frongoch, North Wales.

When we heard this news we were delighted, and I remember on that day, when I met Gearóid O'Sullivan in the prison ring, he presented me with a copy of *The Imitation Of Christ*. He gave it to me as a token of friendship in remembrance of our imprisonment together. I have it still, and prize it highly. He wrote upon the fly-leaf:

"Gearóid O'Sullivan, 44 Mountjoy Street, Dublin,and Block L.1. Richmond Barracks, and Wandsworth Prison. C.2. No. 48. Presented to B.O'Connor, Wandsworth, July 1916".

Each prisoner was served with an Internment form. Mine was as follows:
"Notice to persons with respect to whom an order is made under Regulation 14B.

Name of Prisoner.	Batt. O'Connor.
Address of Prisoner.	1, Brendan Road,
	Donnybrook.

W.O.number   976D.

H.O. "314.204.

"Notice is hereby given to the above named that an Order has been made by the Secretary of State under Regulation 14 B. of the Defence of the Realm Regulations directing that he shall be interned at the place of Internment at Frongoch.

"The Order is made on the grounds that he is of hostile association *and a member of an organization called the Irish Volunteers or an Organization called the Citizen Army, which have promoted armed insurrection against his Majesty.*

"If within seven days from the date of his receiving this notice the above named prisoner submits to the Secretary of State, any representations against the provisions of the said order, such representations will be referred to the Advisory Committee appointed for the purpose of advising the Secretary of State with respect to the internment and deportations of aliens and presided over by a Judge of the High Court, and will be duly considered by the Committee."

CHAPTER XVI

Internment In Frongoch Prison Camp. Release

All the prisoners, with one exception, accepted and signed a receipt for the order. The exception was Henry Dixon, the solicitor. He was removed from Wandsworth and sent, as well as I remember, to Reading Jail.

We had marched into Wandsworth Prison singing *The Soldiers' Song*, and we sang it again as we entered Frongoch.

When we arrived at the camp we were surprised to see no sign of the prisoners and we learned afterwards that they were always confined to the huts whenever a new batch was expected.

We were taken to the Stores Depot where supplies were handed out to us. Each man was given his bed and bedding, knife, fork, spoon, and enamel mug. He was told which hut he was to occupy.

In my hut there were already about twenty-five men. Each hut, when full, held about thirty prisoners. We elected a hut leader. Mine was James Sheils, now an Officer in the National Army.

The Frongoch camp had been erected originally for German prisoners of war. It was in two sections. One, known as the South Camp, was an old disused distillery. The other, the North Camp, consisted of wooden huts which had been specially built. We took our meals in one of the huts which was set apart for the purpose. It was known as the dining-hall.

Life in Frongoch was a very agreeable change after Wandsworth. We had plenty of room to walk about, but, with the bad weather and the thousands of men tramping continually over the same ground, it soon got into the condition of a ploughed field.

We were allowed to receive letters and to write one each week. Our camp leader was M W. O'Reilly who was an officer in the Volunteers and had held command during Easter Week in a position in O'Connell Street, opposite the GPO. Owing to some labour trouble in the Camp the military authorities suspected him and he was transferred to Reading Jail. We then elected Edward Morcan, now a Colonel in the National Army. We had also as camp leader, Séumas Murphy, now our Dublin City Commissioner. It was here I met Séamus Dolan, now TD for Co. Leitrim, and Joint Treasurer with me of the Cumann na nGaedheal Organization.

We had another splendid man with us in Frongoch—Seán Hales of Ballinadee near Bandon. There was not a finer or handsomer man amongst us than he. He was a thorough Irishman of the best type, quiet and unassuming, and full of droll and delightful stories which he told as only an Irishman can. He was a magnificent athlete, far and away the best hammer-thrower in the camp. He could beat his best opponent, not by feet but by yards. It was his assassination during the Civil War which led to the execution in Mountjoy Jail of Liam Mellows, Rory O'Connor, Richard Barrett and Joe McKelvey.

Michael Collins was a prisoner in Frongoch. His hut was opposite mine, across the road. He reminded me that we had met before, and then I recalled that I had seen him at Kimmage, just outside Dublin, a few weeks before the Rising. He had come out there to see the men who had come over from London for the fight, most of whom were known to him. They had arrived ahead of time and had had to be put up somewhere on the quiet. They were housed in a disused mill in Kimmage. I happened to be carrying out some brickwork and alterations for Rory O'Connor, who was an engineer newly returned from Canada. My workmen were setting boilers for him in connection with some engineering project of his. He was not at that time in the Volunteer movement.

Michael Collins looked only a young lad that day in Kimmage. He looked less than his twenty-six years. He was of slight build and boyish appearance.

In Frongoch he was full of fun and mischief. Wherever he was, there were always ructions and sham fights going on. Mock battles took place between the men of his hut and those of the adjoining one. We had a football field and whenever there was a game he was sure to be in it. He was all energy and gaiety. Being a much younger man than myself, we did not at that time become very intimate.

A fellow-prisoner in my hut was James Mulcarnes. He was known as the Rajah of Frongoch. He was a fine singer and comedian and took a leading part in all our concerts. He sang afterwards regularly at the Sinn Féin céilidhí of 1918 and the following years.

John O'Mahony was interned in the South Camp, and he and I did not meet until we were on our way to London for examination before the Advisory Committee. The leader of the South Camp was Michael Staines whom I have already mentioned in connection with the ten-foot pikes. He was a splendid Irishman and an excellent soldier. He had held a responsible position in a large ironmongery business in Dublin but when he became quartermaster of the Dublin Brigade, realizing it would require his whole-time service, he had determined to leave his civil employment. His employer was surprised when he gave notice of his intention and asked him what his grievance was. Michael had none, and had had to invent an excuse, saying that he was going into partnership with me in the building trade, so that several people had congratulated me on the growing success of my business.

We spent a great part of our time in the Irish language classes which were kept going constantly in Frongoch. Michael Lynch, (who is now chief of the Oireachtas Translation Staff), had been most enthusiastic in getting the classes started and he himself taught in them.

In the camp with us were thousands of young men from all parts of Ireland. Some of them had rather hazy ideas of Irish nationality, and had not what we would have thought in Dublin to be a thorough Irish-Ireland outlook.

Frongoch was a splendid school for such young men. The language classes and the example of our zeal and enthusiasm soon rectified this defect in their education. They could not have come to a better school. They were thrown entirely in the company of men to whom national freedom and the old Irish traditions were the highest things in life.

Each day closed with patriotic songs and recitations in which these country fellows loved to join. They were listening all the time to talk and plans about the continuance of the war as soon as we got home. Many a Galway lad who came to Frongoch a harmless gossoon left it with the seeds of Fenianism planted deep in his heart. He went home to become a leader in the subsequent fight. In Frongoch camp were discovered and educated many of the men who afterwards fought the Black and Tans under Michael Collins.

When I say that each day closed with song that is not quite true; it closed with prayer. Our last act at night was to go down on our knees and repeat the Rosary and the Litany of the Blessed Virgin. The Rosary was said every night in every hut in Frongoch camp, not at the command of the camp leader, but out of the impulse to prayer which was in the heart of each of us. Nearly everyone had one or other of the holy images hanging over his bed. A kind friend had sent me a calendar on which there was a sweet picture of the Immaculate Conception. Every night and morning I knelt before it, and when I was released I brought it home with me—that dear companion of my exile. It hangs beside my bed to this day.

One thing at Frongoch greatly impressed us. All the workmen who came to carry out any plumbing or repairs at the camp spoke the Welsh language. This was a great surprise for most of us. We marvelled at the fine national spirit of those men, and their love for their native tongue, that they should have been able to preserve it, and they living alongside the English with not even a bay between.

It gave us a feeling of wholesome humility beside those Welsh fellows to hear them chatting away to each other without a word of English, while we were laboriously re-learning the language of our fathers.

The lesson was not lost on us, and we studied harder than ever in the classes.

The soldiers keeping guard at Frongoch were very friendly. They smuggled out and posted for us any letters we did not want to go through the censor's hands. After a while this was discovered and the guard was changed, but the new guard was not two days in the place before some approached us telling us they were ready to oblige us, and asking to be put in the way of *"earning a tip"*. We did not disappoint them.

The British Government had set up what they called an Advisory Committee to deal with the cases of the interned Irish prisoners. We were one by one brought up before this Committee, who interviewed us in alphabetical order of our names. I being an O'Connor was fairly far behind in the queue. Before me came O'Brien, and after me O'Keeffe, and then O'Mahony. My turn came in August, and I was taken to London with some others. While awaiting the interview, we were lodged in Wormwood Scrubs prison. I found this a miserable place, all the more unpleasant after the comparative freedom of our life in Frongoch.

My interrogation took no more than a few minutes. The members of the Committee adopted a very friendly attitude, addressed me as *"Batt"*, and asked me to take a seat. They asked me if I were married, and the number of my family.

"How was it that you went down to Kerry at that particular time, Batt?"

"I went to see my mother. I liked to visit her at Christmas and Easter, if I could".

"Naturally! It is reported that you were a constant visitor at Tom Clarke's".

"I was. I bought my tobacco and newspapers at his shop, and I liked to have a chat with him about America. We had both lived there for a number of years."

They thanked me for my replies and said I could retire. Seeing them so friendly, I asked if I could expect soon to be released, and I got a nod of assent from the Chairman.

William O'Brien, the Labour Leader of Liberty Hall, had been examined immediately before me. I had met him outside the door as I was going in. He was rather excited. He had adopted a fighting attitude before the Committee, and had been sent to wait in an ante-room *"to think things over"*. *"They are putting things up to me, Batt"*, he said, *"which I have got to consider".*

It was quite plain that the examination was a mere formality, and that the British authorities had made up their minds to get rid of all the Irish prisoners, except those who had been actually caught 'red-handed' in the fight. I daresay they were finding it rather difficult to keep us prisoners while they were fighting a war for the freedom of small nationalities in other parts of

Europe.

We were removed in the evening back to Wormwood Scrubs, and in the seclusion of my cell I wrote two letters, one to my wife, and the other to my mother, telling them that I expected to be home soon, and giving them an account of what had taken place at my interrogation.

These were letters which, obviously, I could not send through the usual prison channels, and I decided to try another way. The next day, on our way back to Frongoch we were taken through London by a private bus to the railway station. There was an armed guard inside and outside. My seat was on top. I had my two letters addressed in my pocket, but I had no stamps. Outside a house, in a street in which there were a number of people, I saw two girls standing and, drawing out the letters, I flung them in their direction. The bus was immediately pulled up, and one of our guard, jumping off, questioned the girls, demanding the letters from them which they refused to give up.

I could not see very well what was happening, but I was not disappointed in my hope. Both my letters duly reached their destination with the necessary stamps attached to them.

I shall never know the names of those two young women, or anything about them. I could not even describe them, but they are warmly in my memory as two who were my friends.

I was not long back in Frongoch before I was given my liberty, and a travelling ticket back to Dublin. I had not time to inform my wife that I was on my way home.

So one early morning in September 1916, I knocked at the door of my house in Brendan Road, and I will not try to describe that meeting, and my happiness to have my family around me once more.

But one trifling incident I would like to record. My little boy, Brendan, had sent me letters, enclosed with his mother's, while I was in jail. He was taking care of a pet of mine, a skylark, which I had had in a cage for some years. His letters consisted of a drawing of the cage and the little bird, with the words in his childish hand, *"The bird is well"*.

On that first morning, he sat listening to all I had to say, and I noticed him watching me. When I had finished my story, he said to me: *"Dadda, now you have been let out of prison, shouldn't we let out our little bird?"*

So that was my first good deed on getting home. Going outside the house I opened the tiny door of the cage, and gave my lark his liberty.

CHAPTER XVII

Sinn Féin And
Reorganization Of The Volunteers

After a week's rest it was time to think of work. I set out to look up my old customers, to let them know that I was free once more, and ready to resume business.

But I got some surprises. There were many who would no longer employ me. The manager of a big firm of whisky bonders, with whom I had a contract to keep their buildings in repair, told me they had no intention of doing business with a *"rebel"*. Others for whom I had worked, while they refused to employ me any more, did not deprive me of what advantage I could get from their opinion. They were surprised, they said, that such a sensible man as I seemed to be should have mixed himself up with *"that Rebellion"*.

Yet I persevered. And though I lost some of my old clients I got new ones, and gradually built up my business once more.

On getting home, I also paid a visit to the tenant of my house in Eglinton Road to collect arrears of rent from him. He had refused to pay the rent to my wife while I was in jail. He had told her that she had no power of attorney to act for me, and she was deprived of this part of my income which I had counted upon her receiving to help to support herself and the children.

I waited my opportunity to get my own back on this fellow, and my chance came a few years afterwards. In 1921 the lease of the house fell in, and he wrote to inform me of the decorations he wished done, preparatory to renewing the lease.

I called to see him.

"I am going to be short and sweet with you", said I. *"I want you to get out"*.

"You are certainly short, but I do not see where the sweetness comes in. You cannot turn me out under the present law."

"I understand the law well enough in the matter", I replied. *"I am in a position to offer you another residence. With my family growing up, my house in Brendan Road is no longer big enough for us, but it will do all right for you. I am going to move in here"*.

I did not fail to enjoy his discomfiture at this change in our situations, and his disgust that the house of a despised *"rebel"* should be considered good enough for him. He did not accept my offer, but moved elsewhere.

Soon after my release, Mrs. Tom Clarke sent for me to tell me that some writings had been found on the walls and door jambs of the house in Moore

Street where Tom Clarke had slept his last night before the surrender. She asked me if I could have them carefully removed and preserved as they were her husband's last message to his countrymen. I had the whole square of plastering cut out intact and encased in a frame with a glass front so that the writing would not get defaced.

This was the message: *"We had to evacuate the GPO The boys put up a grand fight, and that fight will save the soul of Ireland"*.

The other words were on the same note, all glorying in the fact that another blow had been struck for Irish freedom.

I was not inactive in other ways. My misfortunes had not taught me 'sense', and, as soon as I had my business in hand again, I looked up my comrades with a view to our putting into execution the schemes of reorganization we had planned in Frongoch.

We had to keep things going until the penal servitude men were released, amongst whom were, obviously, the men who were to become our new leaders. We had to reap the harvest of the sympathy and enthusiasm which were beginning to spread over the country. We had also to overhaul the National Aid Association, which had been set up to collect funds and distribute them for the benefit of the prisoners and their dependents. We had found, on getting home, that the money was not going to the right people. Those who were best entitled to relief were getting little or none, and others were being helped from the fund who had no claim.

It was decided to hold a meeting of the released men who would naturally be in the best position to know who were the most deserving, and to choose a secretary from amongst them. A few of us, who had already got an idea of the ability of Michael Collins, agreed that we would put his name forward at the meeting.

It was held one night in a hall in Exchequer Street. The crowd was so large that to make room for everyone we all had to stand. When the Chairman asked for names for the secretaryship, several voices called out *"Michael Collins"*. He was still very little known, and his name caused some surprise and questions as to who he was.

We carried his election, and we were justified in our choice. He made a brilliant success of the Association, he became known as a man of great energy and efficiency, and he got to know and be known by all the fighting men. In the National Aid Association he set an example of work, and devotion to duty, which was at first the terror, but soon became the admiration, of everyone who came in contact with him. He had no use for slackness or half-hearted methods, and he would listen to no excuses. He set a standard which we could not but aspire to reach, and which was to bear good fruit afterwards.

We had also to build up again a military organization. Those of us who were strong in the Fenian faith gathered together as best we could the fragments of the IRB.

The circle to which I belonged met once a month, on a Sunday morning in the rooms of the Keating Branch of the Gaelic League at 46 Parnell Square.

Cathal Brugha was opposed to the resurrection of the Organization and Michael Collins was strongly in favour of it. Looking back, I now see this difference of opinion as the first indication of an opposition which was to last between these two men, both intensely sincere patriots, and which was to have such tragic consequences.

Cathal knew that I was again an active member, and in a conversation with me he gave me his opinion that the IRB was *"a spent force"*. I already knew him well enough not to argue with him. Once he made up his mind he never changed it. He was unbending, and, once he decided he was right, he would listen to no one who held an opposite view to his own.

Diarmuid O'Hegarty and Michael Foley were the two most active members of the circle which met in Parnell Square.

Michael Collins was all the time attending to the recruiting side. He was getting together, so far as possible, an active service unit for every area. He was forming his Intelligence Staff, recruited from what was to become the famous Dublin Brigade, which was to destroy the British Secret Service and defeat the Black and Tans. He was full of enthusiasm and hope. He said that the fight had only begun, and that the real struggle lay ahead.

It was the public who, during the Rising, had given us the name *"Sinn Féiners"*. It was the only one they knew to call us by, and though, at that time many of us looked upon Sinn Féin as something which meant only passive resistance, and *"Buy Irish Goods"*, yet when the name was thrown at us as a reproach we accepted it.

And now it was to give us an organization which was to be of enormous strength to us, and without which our military organization would have had no background. But Arthur Griffith was still in prison, and all we could do was to keep things going.

An opportunity soon arose, however, to test the feeling in the country. A by-election occurred in North Roscommon, and we decided to put forward Count Plunkett as the Sinn Féin candidate. He had been released from prison, and, being the father of one of the executed leaders, he made a great appeal to the people, who were now beginning to see in the dead heroes of Easter Week the lineal descendants of Wolfe Tone, Robert Emmett and Lord Edward

Fitzgerald. He was elected, though he had put no settled policy before the voters, and, until he returned to Dublin, we did not even know ourselves whether he meant to go over to Westminster or not.

However, he did not keep us long in the dark. He was met at the Broadstone Station by an enormous crowd. They formed into a procession to lead him in triumph through the streets, and at the head of Dominick Street the procession halted. From the outside car on which he was seated, Count Plunkett addressed the crowd. His speech was short but to the point.

He declared he would never enter the English Parliament. *"The fight will be made in Ireland and won in Ireland"*, he said. *"It will never be won in Westminster"*.

This statement was received with great cheering and enthusiasm.

Michael Collins had been a very active worker in Roscommon. He, too, was in the procession, at the tail end, also on an outside car. As he was passing in front of a public-house in Mountjoy Street, a half-drunken sailor, on leave off a man-of-war, rushed out. He was apparently aware of the nature of the procession, and he called out to Michael Collins: *"If you are a Sinn Féiner come down off that car and I'll fight you"*. He had no sooner said the words than Michael was facing him, with his fists ready. But the sailor changed his mind, and proposed to argue the point. *"Come away, Michael"*, said I, happening to be near him, *"he is not worth your notice"*.

Count Plunkett's victory was followed by the the election of Joe McGuinness for Longford. We posted the constituency with pictures of the candidate sitting in prison clothes within the gates of a jail. Under the picture in large words were: *"Put him in to get him out"*.

When the prisoners were released in June they held a meeting to elect a leader. The name of Tomás Ashe was suggested. But he was of a shy, unassuming nature, and he begged to be excused. *"I can serve Ireland as well in the ranks"*, he said.

It was he who had led the fight at Ashbourne, Co. Dublin, in Easter Week, one of the most striking engagements of the Rising. He held the rank of Commandant, and captured about sixty of the Royal Irish Constabulary, including their officers, during the engagement. He was a tall, very handsome man, over six foot high, with auburn hair. He was a delightful character, full of kindness. He had an intense love for the Irish language. He was musical, and had written several poems. He was a sweet singer of Irish ballads and would sing and recite to us each evening during the week he spent with us in Brendan Road after his release. His last poem, published after his death—*Let Me Carry Your Cross For Ireland, Lord*—made a deep impression, and was repeated everywhere. He was arrested again at the end of that week while on his way to spend another night with us. It was a Saturday evening in August 1917. Michael Foley, already mentioned, was with him. On the previous evening, his last night of freedom, he had delighted us with several songs of his own composition.

After his arrest, he died while on hunger strike from the effects of forcible feeding. On his death, Harry Boland called out to see me. He told me that, as one of Tomás Ashe's greatest friends, I was to help to put his body into uniform for burial. I performed that sacred duty with pride and sorrow, assisted by Maurice Collins, another great friend. Although he had been dead for many hours his limber body was still warm, his splendid young physique being in the full strength and beauty of manhood.

All that, however, was afterwards.

On Tomás refusing to accept the leadership, de Valera's name was proposed. He was elected, to the satisfaction of everyone. He had been the only OC to escape execution, and the senior officer to survive the Rising. He had been the last leader to surrender.

A vacancy then occurred in Clare, and de Valera went down as Sinn Féin candidate, accompanied by Eoin MacNeill. He was elected with a majority which surpassed all our greatest expectations.

We also fought an election in Kilkenny with William Cosgrave, who is now President of the Saorstát (Free State) as our candidate. He had been sentenced to death after the Rising, the sentence being commuted to penal servitude for life.

I went down to help with the canvassing and had with me my old friend of prison days, John O'Mahony. The Irish Parliamentary Party were frantic over our successes, seeing the end of their power in the country, and they put forth their whole strength in Kilkenny to defeat us. They attacked us with the greatest bitterness. They called us *Rainbow Chasers*, and said that our flag suited us with all the colours of the rainbow in it. Yet the people preferred us and Cosgrave was elected.

The next contest took place in S. Armagh in February 1918. We put forward Dr. Patrick McCartan, afterwards an envoy of ours in the USA.

In company with Séumas Dolan of Leitrim, and Seán McEntee, I went down to the constituency. I canvassed and spoke in the Lislea district. Seán O'Muirthuile was in charge of this area, and it was there he began to gain the experience which he put to such excellent use afterwards.

In Armagh we found the Hibernians (the organization of the Irish Parliamentary Party) intensely hostile to Sinn Féin. Were it not for the Limerick and Clare Volunteers whom we drafted into the county we could not have done our work at all. The Volunteers acted as a protection body, keeping order.

So furious were the Hibernians against us that they joined forces with their old political enemies in order to destroy us. On polling day I saw them mingling with the Orangemen, and the two parties marched as one body to vote at Forkhill Polling Station against Dr. McCartan. There is a large Orange vote in Armagh and our candidate was defeated.

This was our first set back, and we felt it sorely. I travelled back to Dublin next day with Piaras Beaslai, and we were full of disappointment over our defeat.

After the S. Armagh election, the Castle authorities began to watch the prominent men in the Sinn Féin organization. Special detectives were employed to spy upon their movements. They were known to us as the political detective squad.

Michael Collins was arrested in Dublin, in April 1918, for a speech he had delivered in Co. Longford. I was on O'Connell Bridge when he was taken, and saw him marched off a prisoner by a number of Dublin Metropolitan Police and detectives. With his arrest, things fell very flat, as already he had become the most indispensable man in the movement and nobody could take his place, and when he had been in prison for a while he gave bail and was released.

That Michael Collins should give bail made many people realize, for the first time, what an important man he was. At that time, men who were arrested for minor activities could get out on their own bail, and Michael Collins was at all times against the idea of men staying in prison who had important work to do outside. On a later occasion, when one of his best Intelligence officers, Tom Cullen, was arrested, he sent him word to give bail and come out. But so strong was the feeling against anything that might seem like knuckling under to the English, that Tom refused to stir till he got the order in writing from his Chief. He got it, in Mick's uncompromising language.

CHAPTER XVIII

Beginning Of My Friendship
With Michael Collins

On the release of Arthur Griffith the headquarters of the Sinn Féin Organization were set up at No. 6 Harcourt Street. My old friend Paddy O'Keeffe was the Secretary. There was never a better man for such a job. He had not only a profound knowledge of the whole movement, but an amazing memory for people, facts, dates, and information of all kinds.

And he knew, as no one else knew, how to deal with callers, and how to protect Griffith from the invasions of curious inquirers. In a back room, Griffith edited *Nationality*, and as he was now becoming known as the founder of Sinn Féin, newspaper men from Ireland, England, America, and other countries were continually calling, hoping to secure an interview. In the front room Paddy dealt with all but the most important, and there was no man in the movement who could have told them more—if he wished.

On one occasion, a very swell-looking fellow with an English accent called asking to see Mr. Griffith. Paddy told him that Mr. Griffith could not be disturbed. Could he help him? The visitor explained that his business was most important. Pressed for particulars, he said he represented a distinguished publishing company, and had been commissioned to write a full-page article on the Irish situation. He wanted to know about Sinn Féin.

"If that is your errand", said Paddy, as he sat on the table dangling his legs, *"I can tell you as well as anyone"*.

A conversation followed, but the visitor was still unsatisfied.

"What is Sinn Féin? What is its ultimate object, Mr. O'Keeffe?"

By now Paddy had grown tired of his stylish visitor. He turned round slowly in his chair, and looked him steadily in the eye. There was a spark of fire in Paddy's own which would have been a danger signal to those who knew him.

"What is our ultimate object, you want to know? Why! vingeance! by ——! vingeance!"

Paddy has a flow of language and richness of expression remarkable even in Ireland. It never runs dry. He has also a more vivid vocabulary than any man I know; and he, too, can be short and sweet.

One day in May 1919 I looked in at No. 6 to have a chat with Páidín (as we call him). I was with him only a few minutes when Seán McGlynn called and handed Paddy a slip of paper.

When he was gone, Paddy said to me, confidentially:

"This is from a friendly detective, Batt. He says there is great activity at the Castle, and all the G. men are notified to report themselves to-night. He thinks there are going to be arrests on a large scale, and the important men had better not sleep at home."

But we had had such alarms before, and we did not act upon the message.

That was the night of the *"German-Plot"* round-up, a plot which was hatched in Dublin Castle, and which none of us heard about until we read of it in the newspapers.

Paddy was arrested with seventy or eighty others, among whom were de Valera and Arthur Griffith.

Michael Collins escaped arrest. He was cycling home when he noticed a military lorry outside his lodgings, and soldiers on the footpath. He guessed what was up, and, continuing on unconcernedly past the house, he turned into the next street, where he knocked up J.J. Walsh to give him warning. He called on a few more who were likely to be arrested, until he came to the house of Seán McGarry; but Seán was already taken. Here he found, however, a safe shelter for himself. *"I knew"*, he told me afterwards *"that having been there already, and arrested Seán, they would not call again"*. So he stayed at McGarry's until the round-up was over.

Paddy O'Keeffe was sorely missed. Harry Boland and James O'Meara were appointed Secretaries of the Sinn Féin Organization in his place, and with the arrest of nearly all the leading men a new situation arose.

Michael Collins now came to the forefront of the whole revolutionary movement. The control of all the important departments came into his hands, and he was not only, by his genius, perfectly well able to perceive and execute what had to be done, but the movement as a whole was enormously strengthened by the various branches being co-ordinated and directed by a single powerful mind.

The Castle officials became aware of him. They put on their most experienced detectives to catch him, and supplied each with his photograph— an old one, fortunately, which was no longer a good likeness.

His office was watched. He gave it up, and came and worked at my house in Brendan Road for a few weeks. But I was known, and it was not safe for him to stay with me for very long. When he left, he moved to Pearse's old school in Oakley Road, but he continued to come daily to Brendan Road for dinner.

It was during these few weeks when we saw each other every day, and spent many hours each evening together, that my intimacy with him became established. We got to know each other thoroughly. I will put it in a nutshell—we trusted each other, and from mutual confidence come all good things in friendship. It was not that we ever gave expression to our feelings for each other. It was not his way to be demonstrative, or to speak of what was in his heart, but the grip of his hand occasionally at parting, (we never shook hands conventionally), told me all I wished to know. It was now that I came fully to know his strength and his faith, his courage and devotion, and I knew that he would turn to me when he wanted one in whom he could put complete confidence. It became my pride to co-operate with him, and to obey his orders. He had only to say *"Look here, Batt..."*

A warm friendship had sprung up between him and Harry Boland. They were about the same age, and they were both high-spirited, unconventional and of convivial habits. While he always got on well with men, Michael Collins was naturally shy in what is called society, and the gay, irresponsible, easy-mannered company kept by Harry was congenial to him. He found relaxation in it. But with his intellectual outlook growing, and his taste and judgment developing rapidly, he also began to seek and enjoy the company of thoughtful people who could respond to and appreciate the new ideas which came crowding upon his mind. He never changed, however, from his dislike of formality.

Harry Boland was also of a daring nature, loving dangerous enterprises for their own sake. Michael had him with him when he planned the rescue of de Valera from Lincoln Jail in January 1919, and the escape was carried out between them.

About this time they occupied a room in my house for about a week. They were both now 'wanted' men, and one morning, while they were at breakfast, my wife went up to see about the making of the beds. She found a revolver under each pillow.

It was then that we fully realized the situation.

"Batt", she said to me, *"those boys will not be taken without a fight"*.

At this time a prominent official attached to the engineering department of the Dublin Corporation was doing some business with me. He called one day with his wife to Brendan Road and we were in the middle of a discussion about wall-papers and paints when Michael Collins, pushing his bicycle, came in through the gate. We could see him passing the sitting-room window on his way to the back door. My visitor sat up in his chair, suddenly on the alert. Peering out, he said:

"That looks like Michael Collins".

"It is Michael Collins", said I, *"would you like to meet him?"*

He did not answer my question, and his wife nervously interjected: *"Dear,*

I am afraid we are keeping Mr. O'Connor. Let us be going. He will have business to do with Mr. Collins".

      "Not at all", said I, *"he has come here for his dinner. I am in no hurry".*

      But they would not stay. *"We can finish our business another time. We couldn't dream of keeping you".* And they hurried away.

That timid gentleman was afterwards an opponent of the Treaty. I met him early in 1922 in the Munster and Leinster Bank. Expanding his chest and assuming a heroic posture, he told me that nothing less than a Republic would satisfy him.

      "Right you are!" said I. *"But before setting up a Republic we'll have to beat the English out of Ireland. The day is not long past when I saw you slinking out of my house"*, I cried, seizing him by the lapel of his coat, *"because Michael Collins was under the same roof with you, and by God, if we are to fight again, I'll see to it that you have a rifle in your hand. You'll be the first man I'll commandeer".*

CHAPTER XIX

Success Of Féin And Establishment Of Irish Revolutionary Government

In November 1918 the General Election had taken place. Sinn Féin swept the country, winning seventy-three seats out of the total of one hundred and five, and the whole position in Ireland was changed.

Sinn Féin had got a clear mandate. Our candidates had told the people that if elected they would not go to the English Parliament, but would stay and look after their interests at home.

So they went ahead to carry out their election promises and to put into force Arthur Griffith's policy of Sinn Féin. They set up *Dáil Eireann*, establishing Ministries, and appointing Ministers, and the people gave their allegiance to the new national revolutionary Government, obeying its behests. English Government being gradually displaced, Castle Rule was now revealed as nakedly military and oppressive. Michael Collins was appointed Minister for Finance. He had been elected TD for his native county without Opposition. He was at this time twenty-eight years of age.

At first the English tried to destroy Dáil Eireann by ridicule. Every day its newspapers referred to it with jokes and sneers. But the infant Government early showed signs of a hardy constitution, and, since it was not to be killed so easily, other measures were determined on.

They set out to destroy it by direct attack. They declared it illegal, and raids were begun for the arrest of its Ministers.

With the establishment of Dáil Eireann, the Volunteers had become the Irish Republican Army, known as the IRA. The English set out to suppress Dáil Eireann. The Volunteers prepared to defend it.

That was how the war began.

To arrest the leaders it was necessary to be able to identify them. For this purpose the English had their instruments: in Dublin, the Detectives (G. men) of the Dublin Metropolitan Police; in the country, the men of the Royal Irish Constabulary (the RIC).

Without these spies—men whose business it was to know every prominent man in the Sinn Féin movement, and every leader of the IRA. in Dublin and throughout the country, and, so far as possible, every man in the rank and file—an English army coming to Ireland to deal by force with a political situation, was powerless

With these spies we were at their mercy, and no effective resistance was possible, as had been proved repeatedly in the past history of our struggle. It was mainly because we had hesitated hitherto to deal with these men that we had so long failed to achieve our end.

We hesitated no longer.

Michael Collins, besides being Minister for Finance, was also Director of Intelligence. He created the Intelligence Department, and took charge of the whole of this part of our defence; and, as this was in fact our main offensive by which we met and outwitted the enemy, he was the man who led the war, who planned and saw executed its most important activities, and who is responsible for its success.

The English were not slow in discovering this. They soon observed that whatever arrests were made, and whatever men put out of action, while Michael Collins was at large everything went on just as well or better (or worse from their point of view).

They also became aware of his hand behind the elimination of their agents. They found themselves up against an opposing Secret Service which was more than a match for their own. In all our previous struggles such a stand-up to them had never been made or even attempted, and they became venomous.

It was borne in upon them that his was the daring, indomitable mind behind our defence, the strength of which they were beginning to feel; and it was then—in 1919—that it was decided that, if caught, he was not to be arrested but shot. His picture appeared in the *Hue And Cry* (a police publication), with a short description of him, ending with the words: "A dangerous man. *Care should be taken that he does not shoot first*"

All meetings of Dáil Eireann had now to be held in secret. The Departments had to carry on their work in hidden offices, and all important commands and instructions had to be conveyed privately by trustworthy messengers.

At one of those early meetings it was suggested that members who had been recently released from prison after hunger strike should not attend the Dáil. It was feared that in their poor state of health they might not be able to stand another term of imprisonment, and it was always possible that the place of meeting might be discovered and raided. Arthur Griffith spoke, supporting the proposal, but added that there was one member who had not been in prison lately, yet whose arrest would be disastrous.

> "*I refer to Michael Collins*", he said, describing him as "*the dynamo of the whole movement*".

This tribute from a man of the cool judgment of Arthur Griffith was the first indication to many of the position now reached by Michael Collins.

Money was needed for the new Administration and for carrying out the plans of reconstruction agreed to by Dáil Eireann, and, as Minister of Finance, Michael Collins raised the Dáil Loan of 1919-1920. He asked for £250,000, but, in fact, £400,000 was subscribed, and of this £25,000 was in gold.

"Bring it to me in gold, Batt", he said, when I went to him with the subscriptions I had collected.

I obeyed. I got shopkeepers and business men whom I knew, to hoard every sovereign and half sovereign which came into their hands, and I exchanged notes for the gold from time to time.

When the Loan closed in July 1920, the gold was entrusted to me, to be put into a safe hiding-place. The Loan of course had been declared illegal, and anyone found and convicted of subscribing to it or collecting for it was imprisoned. But while this did not interfere with its success, (quite the contrary), it meant that if any of the money had been discovered it would have been confiscated.

Doctor Fogarty, Bishop of Killaloe, a splendid patriotic Irishman, and one of our truest friends, was one of the many trustees, and I think Lord Monteagle was another. The main fund in notes was banked in their names; and the gold—packed in four boxes each weighing about two cwt., and a baby's coffin—was placed in my keeping.

I worked all night alone burying the boxes beneath the concrete floor of my house in Brendan Road. Lying on my side, I had to work myself forward beneath the floor. Backwards and forwards I moved wriggling like a worm, upon my hip and elbow, bringing one box at a time, pushing it in front of me in the confined two foot space between the cement floor of the house and the wooden floor of the room under which I worked.

I was gasping for want of air, and pouring with sweat, so that early in my work I had stripped myself nearly to the skin. It took me seven hours to complete the job. One of my difficulties was having so little room to raise my arm to any height before bringing down my hammer to break through the concrete foundation. But I persevered, and having dug the necessary cavities and buried the boxes, I made good the concrete again.

I did the work with great care and neatness, and I got my reward, because though the house was raided several times, the appearance of the floor never aroused suspicion. The hiding-place was known only to my wife and myself. Michael never asked me where I had hidden the gold. He knew it was in the safest place I could think of, and that was all he cared about.

It remained undisturbed until September 1922, when, shortly after his death, I was requested by the Accountant-General of Dáil Eireann, George

McGrath, to produce the boxes so that the gold could be deposited in the vaults of the Bank of Ireland.

This was done in the presence of the Accountant-General. Fourteen bank clerks counted the money after the Bank was closed to the public at three o'clock. Each box had a tag on the inside, showing the amount it contained, and in each case the figure mentioned on the tag was right to a half sovereign.

The gold coin amounted to £24,957, and some bags containing gold bars and foreign coins were valued at £114. A receipt was given by the Bank to the Accountant-General for this total—£25,071.

That was very soon after Michael was killed, and while we were still stricken with desolation at his loss. That day in the Bank, looking at those labels which he had touched with his own hands, I felt that we were back again in the first days of our mourning. I saw him, in my imagination, three years before, in some secluded place, proudly counting and labelling the gold which was to support us in the struggle on which he entered with such hope.

Newspapers were suppressed for advertising the Loan, and in several cases the machinery was dismantled and removed. Patrick Mahon's printing works suffered severely, and he himself was arrested and interned, so that it became almost impossible to get any Sinn Féin literature printed. It was decided, therefore, that we must have a printing press of our own, and we were fortunate in being able to purchase a printing business known as the *General Advertiser and Wood-printing Press*. Towards this venture I subscribed £687, and I know that John McLaughlin (now Senator) subscribed £1,500. I was repaid my contribution in March 1923.

While I was collecting for the Loan I happened to be doing some repairs to the kitchen of a well-to-do house in a suburb of the City, and, as I was always on the look-out for subscribers, I questioned the cook, whom I knew to be a good Irish girl, upon the political opinions of her master. He held a high position in the biggest business concern in Dublin. *"I don't know what he is"*, she said, *"but I have seen some Sinn Féin papers in his room"*.

That was enough for me, and, getting some of the Loan application forms and other suitable literature I sent them to him, adding a note to say that "a collector" would call on the following Saturday afternoon (when my business for the week would be over).

As soon as I was shown into his room on the Saturday, and he recognized me as the man who was doing his repairs, he ran forward to meet me with outstretched hands, his face all aglow.

> *"Ah, Mr. O'Connor"*, he cried, *"why didn't you tell me? So it was you who sent me the papers! I am delighted. Sit down. You must let me get you some refreshment."*

He produced immediately a bottle of whisky and a box of choice cigars. He could not make enough of me. After spending a most agreeable hour with him, I went away with a subscription of £60, and a present of the whole box of cigars which he pressed upon me saying that he never smoked them himself.

But that was not all. Such generosity could not satisfy his ardent, overflowing nature. His position was such that he could not come out openly on our side, so that he could satisfy his patriotic feelings only by lavish munificence. He begged me to call to see him every month. At each visit the same welcome and entertainment were repeated. Each time I left with £50. Sometimes out of mere shyness I would refrain from calling. His kindness was almost over-powering. I felt that his generosity should not be taken advantage of. But he was not to be denied. After waiting a day or two for my expected visit, he would call and leave his subscription at my house.

He was a North of Ireland man and a Presbyterian. He told me once that his grandfather had been a United Irishman, and had suffered for his faith. I think that noble man must have given altogether £650 to the funds of the Revolution. He would make little speeches to me, wishing to make nothing of his self-sacrifice. "I am taking no risks", he would say. *"It is you who are undergoing the dangers—you, and all those splendid young men who are carrying on the fight".*

To my sorrow, he died before the Peace, and I had not the great pleasure to which I had been looking forward, of bringing Michael Collins to see him. That would have been the grandest moment of his life. Whenever he spoke his name during our meetings, it was with awe and emotion.

CHAPTER XX

Growing Power Of Dáil Eireann

The Sinn Féin organisation issued orders, early in 1920, that at the coming Local Government elections candidates should go forward on the Sinn Féin programme, and try to get a majority on the Local Councils.

I stood for Pembroke and was elected, and in the following January, 1921, I was made Chairman of the Council. The next morning Michael Collins called in for a moment to congratulate me on becoming the *"Mayor of Pembroke"*. He was pleased, he said, to see me the Chairman of the second most important Urban Council in Ireland.

About this time extra military were drafted into Dublin. Some of them were billeted in the offices of the Pembroke Council, so that the entire Council staff had to vacate the building at a moment's notice, and we were not allowed even to move our money and our papers. We had to carry on afterwards at the technical schools.

While presiding at a Council meeting one evening, word was passed to me that a military officer had received instructions to arrest me. I slipped away quietly, explaining that I was needed at home owing to the sudden illness of one of my family. It was through a DMP sergeant that I escaped arrest on that occasion.

Another time, this same sergeant, a friendly Kerry man, named O'Hanlon, saved my house from a midnight raid. The military called to his station to get a policeman to guide them to my house, and he persuaded them that they were misinformed. I was a busy building contractor, he said, with no time for anything outside my business.

While I was Chairman of the Council, (an office which I held until 1924, when I was elected to represent Co. Dublin in our native Parliament, *An Dáil*) we had to be very careful that our rates, when lodged in the bank, would not be captured by the Dublin Castle authorities to pay decrees for *"criminal injuries"* awarded by the Courts for damages caused during IRA activities. Our very able Town Clerk, Mr. J.C. Manly, was of the greatest assistance to us in these difficult circumstances.

By 1920, in spite of the fact that the Sinn Féin Government, Dáil Eireann, had been declared illegal by the British authorities, and had to meet and de-liberate and issue its decrees in secret—its Ministers all being 'wanted' men liable to arrest—its administration was growing in prestige and power, and the Sinn Féin Courts were, all over the country, taking the place of the British Courts.

In the Pembroke district we held our Court in a spacious room in the

Ballsbridge Dispensary. It had an entrance from the rear through which we were able to pass into the meeting unnoticed. I was a constant attendant at the Ballsbridge Court. The Courts were held at night. The decisions of the Judges were never questioned, but implicitly accepted and obeyed.

CHAPTER XXI

We Keep Going

I was one of the original shareholders of the National Land Bank which was set up in March 1920 at 68 Lower Leeson Street. Robert Barton, at the direction of Michael Collins, took a very prominent part in its formation. The Bank is now in Dame Street. It was purchased by the Bank of Ireland after the establishment of the Free State.

Bob Barton had been elected for County Wicklow in the General Election of 1918, and became Minister for Agriculture in our first Dáil. He was arrested for a speech he made in Wicklow, and Michael Collins had successfully arranged his rescue from Mountjoy Jail.

On his escape he came to my house for a few weeks, and then moved to the house of Mrs. Eamonn Ceannt in Oakley Road. Mrs. Ceannt, the widow of one of the heroes of Easter Week, was a great worker in the cause. She was a member of the Standing Committee of Sinn Féin. Her sister, Lily O'Brennan, who lived with her, was another who gave most devoted and invaluable help.

I was a constant visitor while Barton was in Oakley Road, and he and I often took runs on our bicycles to Killiney, where he had hundreds of sheep grazing on the golf links. I accompanied him on one occasion on a flying visit to his house in Annamoe. We were both armed, and were ready for anything that came along. But our journey was uneventful, and we returned in safety.

We went sometimes together to see Erskine and Mrs. Childers who were now living in Terenure in a house vacated by Sir John Taylor. Sir John had thought it safer for him to take up his residence in Dublin Castle. I had been given the contract to renovate the house, and make certain alterations.

Barton's movements must have been noted at last for one night the house in Oakley Road was raided. He escaped out of bed in his pyjamas. But the place was surrounded, and he was arrested while getting into another street at the rear of the house.

A second rescue of him was planned by Michael Collins. In view of his former escape he was much too closely guarded in prison to attempt a repetition of the former plan, but it was arranged that on the day of his court martial the military lorry bringing him back to Mountjoy after his trial should be held up.

Michael spoke to me of his plans for the rescue. *"I wonder what would be the best way to make the car pull up"*, he said. I suggested that I should have ready—up a side street—a builder's hand-cart with scaffolding poles and a long ladder. When the lorry was sighted, the signal would be passed on to the men with the hand-cart who would run it out across the street as the lorry approached. The men in ambush could then rush forward and disarm the guard.

All this fell out perfectly according to plan and the lorry was held up in Berkeley Road. But Barton was not in it. The military had taken precautions, and had had him conveyed by another route.

Michael Collins was very sad over this mishap. He had a great regard for Barton, who had broken with his family traditions in coming over to our side. Barton was sentenced to three years' penal servitude and sent to Portland Prison in England. He was released after the Truce. Later, he was selected to be one of the plenipotentiaries who went to London to negotiate the peace. He signed the Treaty, but was opposed to its terms, and made a speech against it during the debates held before its ratification. Subsequently, he took no part on either side, but retired to Annamoe.

In November 1920, I went down to speak at a meeting in Newmarket, Co. Cork. My companions were Madame Markiewicz, and Paddy O'Keeffe, TD for the Division.

We arrived in the town on a Saturday night to find that the meeting had been proclaimed. The town was filled with RIC and British Military. Nevertheless, we held a meeting that night in the street on the stroke of midnight, and when we were ordered to stop by the officer in charge, we stole out of the town, and scouts were sent in all directions to pass round the word that the meeting would be held in Kiskeam instead of in Newmarket. We cut the telephone wires, and a splendid meeting was held in Kiskeam in which several bands took part.

Madame Markiewicz had to make a second speech to satisfy those who arrived late. She roused the greatest enthusiasm by her sincere and burning words. She was at her best describing the Rising of Easter Week, and her own part in it, when, dressed in the Volunteer uniform, she led the men who occupied Stephen's Green, and the College of Surgeons. In her speech that day she repeated the words of The O'Rahilly who was killed in the fighting: *"It is madness"*, he said, *"but it is glorious madness, and I am with you to the last"*.

After the meeting she presented me with her photograph, on which she wrote: *"To my comrade at Newmarket, Batt O'Connor, March 1st, 1920"*. I preserve this memento of this brave and remarkable woman with the greatest care.

CHAPTER XXII

Raids And Escapes

On one occasion when the Sinn Féin headquarters at No. 6 Harcourt Street were raided, Michael Collins was in an upstairs room. He had an office in the building. He succeeded in bluffing the first policeman who came into the room, and passing out leisurely, as if he were an unimportant assistant clerk, he ran lightly up to the floor above and escaped through the skylight.

His papers fell into the hands of the raiders, and No. 6 being now useless he gave me instructions to buy a house which was for sale further up the street—No. 76.

As I was in the building trade it was easy for me to buy houses without arousing suspicion. We had to move cautiously, not only with an eye upon the enemy, but upon the people with whom we did business. With the propertied classes, Sinn Féin naturally was not popular. The owner of a house in Stephen's Green had refused to sell when he discovered that it would be used as one of our offices.

So we learned to keep our own counsel, and when I was commissioned to buy a house for the offices of one of our Departments—and I did nearly all this part of the business—I took care to buy it for *"a client"*, or some *"friend of mine"*, who wanted *"a nice residence in Dublin"* or *"good business offices"*, and the house was purchased in his or her supposed name.

When we had completed the purchase of No. 76 I went to Michael Collins.

> *"Michael"*, said I, *"they raided No. 6, and it is within the bounds of possibility that they will spot and raid No.76. How about my putting in a hiding-place for your papers?"*

He was pleased with the idea, and I found a recess suitable for my purpose in a fitted-in wardrobe in one of the rooms. It was a simple job to partition off a portion of the wardrobe, and, having made it accessible by a secret spring, to repaper the whole while the general papering and repainting was being done.

I also arranged a means of escape for him through the skylight, leaving a light ladder in readiness which he could pull up after him. Two or three doors off there was a hotel, and we took the proprietors into our confidence. They agreed that their skylight should be used in the event of a raid on No. 76. These gentlemen were not of our way of thinking, and it was against their religious principles to take part in any kind of violence, but they were of chivalrous nature, men who would be naturally on the side of the oppressed, and they showed true friendship towards us on this and many other occasions. We also arranged with the boots of the hotel that the skylight should never be bolted.

All these precautions bore good fruit when, before long, No. 76 also fell to the enemy. Michael used the skylights, and dropped into the hotel after nearly breaking his ribs on the rail of the stairs. The skylight happened to be situated immediately over the well of the stairs, so that he had to swing his body backwards and forwards before dropping, and only escaped falling through the well by landing on the rail. He passed out of the hotel as one of the visitors, and, mingling among the crowd in the street, he watched the raid as it proceeded. Then he came to Brendan Road to tell me the news.

A few days before, the rescue from Manchester Jail had taken place, when, planned by Michael Collins, sixteen of our prisoners had escaped over the prison wall. They had remained hidden with friendly Irish families in Manchester, while the hunt for them was going on.—Now, one by one, by various routes, they began to dribble home.

Piaras Beaslai had arrived, one of the first of the prisoners to return, and he was in my house when Michael came in and told us about the raid at 76. That was a very pleasant reunion, and we did not fail to celebrate the happy occasion.

A few days later Austin Stack arrived in Brendan Road, and after him came Seán Milroy, two more refugees from Manchester. Stack's health had suffered in prison, but under the care of Dr. Richard Hayes, an Easter Week man, he soon recovered. He stayed with me for about six weeks, and then Michael sent word that it was not safe for him to stay any longer, upon which he moved to Grand Canal Street to the house of Mrs. Gordon, who afterwards became his wife.

In the raid on No. 76, my secret closet was not discovered. Michael was pleased, and from that day onwards I was the Minister of a special Department all my own. I was entrusted with the construction of all the hiding-places in the various houses we used, and I became quite skilful in devising them, so that valuable lives, and papers upon the preservation of which the success of our fight depended, were kept out of the hands of the enemy.

All the houses in which I built hiding-places were not raided. But in those which were, they stood the test, including the later raids of the Auxiliaries and Black and Tans who were past masters in the art of scientific searching.

Michael Collins had been working in 76 for only about a month or six weeks when it was discovered.

The constant shifting and moving of his papers, which were ever increasing, was becoming a great inconvenience, and he now took some trouble to find a house that would not be likely to attract notice, or arouse suspicion of the use to which it was being put.

He found what he wanted in Mespil Road, a quiet street of small residential houses on the south side of the City. It runs between the two thoroughfares of Baggot Street and Leeson Street. No. 5 is a few doors off the Leeson Street end. In the continual traffic of Leeson Street he could cycle unnoticed, and turning into Mespil Road he was within the hall door in half a minute.

It is a small, two-storied house, and is approached through the usual low gateway and asphalt path, with a strip of grass on the left-hand side in front of the parlour window.

This ground floor parlour was his office. He rented it from the lady who occupied the house with her two daughters. As he sat at his desk behind the lace curtains, his revolver beside him, he could see without being seen any one who approached. At the back of the house were the large grounds of Tullamaine, covering several acres. Through these he could make a quick and safe retreat.

He never slept in this house, nor in any of his offices, and all we had to do was to make a hidden receptacle into which his papers could be quickly pushed. This I did by fixing a small cupboard in the woodwork beneath the kitchen stairs. Before leaving each evening at five o'clock, his papers were hidden away.

This was his War office. His Finance offices were in Mary Street and St. Andrew Street. There he required a fairly large staff of clerks and a busy thoroughfare was more suitable. Not more than five persons knew the Mespil Road address—his two chief Intelligence Officers, Liam Tobin and Tom Cullen, his typist (Miss Mason), Joe O'Reilly, and myself. When I told him that a certain man (one of ourselves, and a distinguished professional man) wanted to see him, he said quickly and decisively:

"I can't see him here, Batt, I can't have this office known by anyone outside the few of us who use it".

It lasted fifteen months, and then in April 1921 it was raided. The raid took place at night, so he was not there. The house was turned upside down, and all the floors were pulled up, and the trimmings of doors and windows pulled down. The search lasted twenty-two hours, but though the woodwork immediately under my cupboard was broken in, nothing was found there, and the cupboard itself was missed. Fortunately I had built it a foot or two above the floor, with a false back, behind which was the hiding-place.

The raiders found two desks, two loaded revolvers, a typewriter, and some Sinn Féin notepaper, but not a written word or document. Yet close at hand were all the files and papers of his Intelligence and Military activities of fifteen months' accumulation.

He had a very narrow escape from capture on this occasion. The raiders waited concealed in the house for his expected arrival in the morning. They removed all signs of their occupation, and, had their hopes been fulfilled, his life would have certainly ended that morning.

But during the night the mother had feigned illness and, after a great deal of reluctance, the raiders had agreed to allow the daughter, accompanied by one of themselves to see that all was *bona-fides*, to go out and get a doctor. While being medically attended to, the mother was able to whisper a word explaining the situation, trusting to the doctor's good will, and begging that a message should be sent at once to John McCluskey, caretaker of the Land Bank, who would know what to do.

I was not, of course, sleeping at home, but word was got to me in time. We could not get into direct touch with Michael though we sent round trusty messengers in haste to all his houses of shelter which we knew. In the morning, therefore, we fell back upon our last resource. At the corners of all roads leading to Mespil Road, we posted scouts. One of them was my little daughter, Eileen. Punctually, Michael was seen to approach and was intercepted.

I saw him later in the day when the raiders, disappointed of their quarry, had at last withdrawn. He greeted me warmly.

> *"Batt, I was greatly afraid they would find the papers, they were in the house for so long. If they had got them, they would have beaten us in a few weeks, as all our plans and our best men would have become known to them".*

That was a proud day for me. It was the first time he had ever praised me. I had once heard him say:

> *"Why should I thank people for doing their part? Isn't Ireland their country as well as mine?"*

It was characteristic of him that of his own narrow escape he had nothing to say.

CHAPTER XXIII

I Am On The Run

I did not sleep at home for fifteen months before the Truce. My house was raided four times during that period. I had two houses of refuge, one round the corner in an adjoining street, and the other three miles away in Terenure.

My first night from home evading arrest was spent at the house of Mrs. Erskine Childers in Wellington Road. I happened to be calling there when I got word that my home had been raided. Mrs. Childers insisted that I should stay and sleep in her house that night. She said she felt it a great privilege to shelter a wanted man.

The house near my own in Donnybrook which I used was raided one night for me. And I should have been there that night, but on that very day I had met with an accident which had necessitated my going to hospital for treatment for concussion. Were it not that I was in hospital, I would certainly have been arrested that night. The raiders told the people of the house that they had trustworthy information that they were sheltering a wanted man. They questioned my friends very closely about their empty spare room. Needless to say, I stayed there no more.

I was unconscious all the first night I was in hospital, and when I came to myself, not knowing where I was, my first words were: *"What is the charge against me?"* During the week I was there, Michael called every evening to see my wife, to show his sympathy, in spite of the danger of visiting a known house like mine.

After a week, fearing the hospital might be raided, he had me removed, sending a taxi for me. He had secured a safe retreat for me in Sandycove, overlooking the sea, where my health was soon restored.

He sometimes slept at No. 23 Brendan Road, one of my houses. At his request, I had given possession of it to Miss O'Connor, aunt of his typist, Miss Mason.

I constructed a secret room in it, and on the occasions when he intended sleeping there, he looked in on me at No. I, on his way. He would arrive half an hour or so before Curfew (at that time ten o'clock), and we would be together at my house till within a couple of minutes of that hour.

We would leave the house together to go to our sleeping quarters. I was often struck by the bold way he would open the hall door, marching out with his head up, and with firm footsteps, the sound of which could be heard through the whole street. Often I was on the point of exclaiming, *"Damn it, man, don't make so much noise"*. Everyone would be under cover and the stillness was profound. He had a small piece of steel on the heel of one of his shoes, and as I walked as quietly as I could, almost tiptoeing round the corner, I would hear his loud footsteps echoing down the whole length of Brendan Road.

This bold, self-confident manner of his often struck me in contrast with the ways of other of our men. They would only leave my hall door with the greatest circumspection, peering round it to see who might be outside, and drawing down their caps well over their eyes before venturing forth. He had a great contempt for these manoeuvres and said such men were asking for trouble.

No. 23 came very near being raided one night when he was there. The military came to search four suspected houses in the Donnybrook district. While raiding the third house on the list, the officer in charge found some love letters belonging to the daughter of the house. She was a girl of spirit, and was indignant with the officer when he began to read them.

> *"What kind of a gentleman are you at all?"* she cried. *"You are not a bit gallant, prying into a poor girl's letters from her sweetheart".*

He was quite abashed. (He was a military officer, not a Black and Tan.)

> *"You are quite right"*, he said, *"it is not cricket"*, and, in his confusion, the slip of paper, on which were written the number and street of the houses to be raided, got mixed in with the letters he returned to her.

When he left the house to go to the next address, not a trace of the missing list could he find.

He crossed the road, and knocking up a chemist's shop where there was a telephone he spoke to Dublin Castle. The chemist was Mr. McElhinney of Morehampton Road, a friend of mine. The officer told of his loss, and asked to have the address of the fourth house repeated. But this the Castle people would not do. McElhinney heard him say to one of the other officers: *"They refuse to give me the address over the 'phone".*

The next morning the young girl came to my house with the missing list. She had found it amongst her letters and she came to warn me. The address on the slip was O'Connor, 23 Brendan Road, and as my house had been raided before, she assumed it was a mistake for No. I.

I sent a message at once to Michael with news of his escape.

But he had other houses in which he was sure of his welcome, though indeed not so very many. It needed a brave woman to shelter Michael Collins. I do not mean that we had not hundreds and thousands of fine, courageous women in Ireland. God forbid that I should forget it. But knowing the terrible risks run by anyone who sheltered him, he himself felt comfortable only in the houses of women of special nerve and self-control. If he felt that the woman of the house was nervous during his stay, he avoided putting her through the ordeal again. And there was another indispensable quality needed. She must be a woman of close tongue, one who would never move her lips to mention his name or his presence in her house.

Mrs. O'Donovan was one of those brave women, and her house in Rathgar was a favourite one of his. Mrs. Lynch, of Walter House, Richmond Road, was another, and he often slept with a brother of Diarmuid Lynch, at the Distillery there.

Mrs. Maurice Collins, of Parnell Street, was another woman whom Michael Collins held in very high esteem for her coolness and bravery. Her place was continually raided both by night and by day, and was, therefore, one which could not be used as a retreat. But she did great service in other ways, and was a most patriotic Irishwoman. I have mentioned Mrs. Paddy O'Keeffe as a very brave woman. Her restaurant in Camden Street was a favourite place where Michael Collins would slip in for lunch. Mrs. Andrew Woods, of Morehampton Road, was another enthusiastic worker who had always a welcome for men on the run. She did great work also in collecting funds for the Prisoners' dependents. Liam Mellows and Seán Etchingham stayed in her house in safety for a long time. Another woman upon whose courage and welcome our hunted men could always rely was Mrs. Liam Devlin of Parnell Street.

These are, of course, only a few of all the fine Irishwomen, most of whose honoured names are well known, who stood by the men during those anxious years.

Before the hunt for him began, Michael Collins lived at the Munster Hotel, Mountjoy Street, kept by Miss McCarthy, a Kerry woman. She was also full of courage and could be deterred by no difficulty or danger. When he could no longer occupy his rooms there, Miss McCarthy continued to look after his laundry, and he went to the house every Sunday, right up to the Truce, to change his linen and underwear. As soon as the Truce was signed, he went back to her house, although he then began to receive pressing offers of hospitality from some of the most fashionable houses in the City.

CHAPTER XXIV

A Narrow Escape

A young man from Cork called to see me one evening on business. He was anxious to find work in Dublin. We sat by the fire talking, not noticing the time passing, as he gave expression to the great enthusiasm he felt for the fight we were making in Dublin.

He longed for the time to come when he could share in the danger and the glory.

"I would live on a meal a day", he said, *"to be among such men"*.

When I looked at my watch I was taken aback to find that it was within a few minutes of Curfew. I explained the position to my young friend. I told him that my home was sometimes raided, and that I was accustomed to sleep elsewhere, and that if he had lodgings to go to, he must set out at once. I added, however, that there was a bedroom to spare if he cared to occupy it, and that I was ready myself to risk sleeping at home for the pleasure of his company for an hour or two longer.

"Certainly, I will stay", he said, still full of enthusiasm. *" If there is a raid, what matter!"*

We went to bed sometime before midnight. I had not been long asleep when I was awakened by my wife. She told me in a whisper that the road was full of soldiers, and that they were coming towards the house.

I had barely time to put on some clothes and scramble into a small hiding-place before the raiders were thundering at the door.

My hiding-place was built in at the back of a small room which was used for holding kitchen utensils. It had a secret door against which leaned sweeping brushes, buckets, and dust pans. As soon as I got in, my wife and my sister quickly and noiselessly replaced the buckets and brushes in position. Immediately afterwards I could hear the sound of running feet all over the house.

The raiding party was in charge of two officers. One officer superintended the search upstairs, and the other took the sitting-rooms, kitchen, and apartments on the ground floor. There were about fifteen men in the house.

The downstairs officer, while his men were ransacking the kitchen, came into the cupboard-room, behind the wall of which I was hidden. The glare of the light of his electric torch penetrated the splits of the little door which separated us so that I was sure he must see me. My hiding-place was so small that I had to crouch inside it in a doubled-up position. The place was cold and I had hardly any clothing on, and if I had inadvertently sneezed or cleared my throat I was undone. And because I knew I must not make the faintest noise, every moment I felt I must, and that I could not control myself any longer.

I lay listening to their voices, and praying that my breathing would not be heard by them. My intense awareness of their nearness made me fancy that they must be aware of mine.

After a while the upstairs officer came down, and he, too, came into the little apartment and examined it with his torch. I heard him moving away the brushes. I was now certain all was over, and I kept repeating my prayers. Then I heard him walk away. He had suspected nothing.

That was the end of the raid, and I listened to the sound of the retreating footsteps, the dying away of all the clamour and noise, and at last the bang of the hall door.

But I was in no hurry to leave my retreat. I was too old and shrewd a soldier to do anything hastily. And I got the reward of my patience. The raiders were not long gone before they came rushing back again. One of the officers had left behind his gloves and his torch. Again the house was searched until they were found where he had left them, on a table in the kitchen.

When they had departed for the second time, and my wife from behind the curtain saw them well away, I ventured forth. She described to me all that had taken place. Our young visitor had been arrested. Found in bed, he was ordered roughly to get up. Trembling, he pleaded for privacy to dress himself. The order was only repeated more roughly: *"No nonsense! Out with you"*.

He was questioned. What was his name? What was he doing in my house?

He answered in great trepidation. As soon as he was dressed he was taken outside, a prisoner, to one of the lorries. He expected to find me beside him among the armed men, and nearly gave me away, it being on the tip of his tongue to ask where I was.

Well, he was kept a prisoner for sixteen days, until his account of himself could be verified and his innocence established. And as soon as he was released, he went straight to Kingsbridge Railway Station, and waited there with feverish impatience until he could get into the first train which was to carry him home. He had lost all enthusiasm for living on a meal a day in Dublin.

On the morning after the raid my wife went through the house to see what damage had been done. She removed the sheets and blankets off our visitor's bed to find beneath the pillow something belonging to him. It was a bottle of holy water!

CHAPTER XXV
Michael Collins's Coolness

One morning I met Michael Collins. He told me, laughing, that he had just been held up.

He was returning from a week-end in the country where he had been attending to military matters. When he reached Ballsbridge he found a cordon of military, who were stopping and searching all incoming cars.

Without waiting to be questioned, he stepped out of his car and walked up to the officer in charge and began to converse with him. They became quite friendly as Michael sympathized with him on the unpleasantness of his job. From a silver cigarette case he offered the officer a cigarette.

While this little comedy was being played, the soldiers were searching the car, and questioning the other men who were in it. Coming back to the officer they saluted: *"Car and passengers all right, Sir"*.

They did not think of searching the man who was talking and laughing with their officer. The papers were in his pockets, documents and maps which would have led to his discovery. *"I was the only one of us who had anything on him"*, he said, *"but thinking I must be a friend of their officer, they never touched me"*.

With a final word of chaff with his new acquaintance he stepped back into the car and continued on his way.

We had rented new offices in Mary Street, a busy thoroughfare, with a constant stream of people passing continually along the pavement, and in and out of the building. He liked such streets, where the presence of two or three fresh faces would pass unnoticed.

He took me with him to look at the place, and to point out to me on the spot certain alterations he wanted made, and where new fittings were to be put in.

As we were walking along the street we met two men of the DMP. He looked them straight in the face, and while they were still watching us, we went into a public-house. We remained there for about ten minutes. To behave in so casual a way was to disarm suspicion.

"Even if they recognized me, Batt, they would be afraid to report they saw me", he said, *"and, supposing they did report it, it would take at least an hour before the necessary force to seize me could be mobilized. And, of course, all the time I would wait here until they were ready to come along! I will tell you something. I do not allow myself to feel I am on the run. That is my safeguard. It prevents me from acting in a manner likely*

to arouse suspicion".

He had set up offices for the different departments of Dáil Eireann—Home Affairs, Finance, Trade and Commerce. They were all in busy streets like Henry Street, O'Connell Street, Bachelor's Walk, Frederick Street, and other frequented thoroughfares, and were situated in buildings where there would be a number of people constantly passing in and out, and where our men and messengers would not be likely to attract special attention. He usually entrusted me with the work of fitting up these offices with electric light, office furniture, new locks with a number of keys, and a brass plate with the name of solicitors who did not exist, so far as we knew, and other invented names of business firms carrying on all sorts of industries and wholesale trade.

We went once together on our bicycles to look at a vacant house at the junction of Upper Leeson Street and Sussex Terrace. I thought the position unsuitable. It stood on the V or junction of two streets, and was in an exposed position. When I pointed this out, he agreed with me, and abandoned the idea of taking it. We purchased instead a house in Wellington Road.

CHAPTER XXVI
Arrival Of The Black And Tans.
I construct Hiding-Places

The war was now at its height.

At a meeting of members of the Dáil, in April 1919, at which Eoin MacNeill presided, an edict was issued that the RIC in every part of the country were to be ostracized and boycotted:

"If Mr. Macpherson may incite the Police, the Irish people as an organized society have a right to defend themselves. They must be made to feel how base are the functions they perform. They are no ordinary Civil Force as police are in other countries. The R.I.C., unlike any police force in the world, is a military body, armed with rifle, bayonet, and revolver, as well as baton. They are given full licence by their superiors to work their will upon an unarmed population."

In consequence, many men of the RIC resigned, and recruiting in Ireland came to a standstill. But it was necessary for the British greatly to increase the strength of their forces, and they were obliged to find recruits in England.

The first of these who came over were known as the Auxiliary RIC (Royal Irish Constabulary), or, more shortly, the Auxiliaries. They were British ex-officers who had fought in the European War, and who came over to fight again for the British Empire by putting down *"rebellion"* in Ireland. They came to Ireland to perform what was for them a patriotic, if unpleasant, duty. They were told who were the most dangerous of the *"rebels"*, and that of these Michael Collins was the leader. He was the head of a *"murder gang"*, and his capture and death would mean the end of the *"rebellion"*, and therefore the safety of the Empire.

So they searched for him everywhere, and knew the personal risks they ran.

His name had become a terror to the British. He had rescued his friends and comrades out of their most impregnable jails; he had eluded all their efforts to capture and kill him; and their cleverest spies, one by one, had been spotted by him, and were dealt with before they had time to achieve success.

The Auxiliaries threw themselves thoroughly into the work of raiding and searching. Whole areas of the City were one after another swiftly surrounded and hemmed in. They were held in a close net for days until the search was finished. Every house within the area was ransacked from attic to cellar. Every person was questioned and searched. The milkman and the baker were searched before being allowed to enter with their provisions, and searched and scrutinized again before being permitted to pass out. Yet no man of any importance was captured during these investments.

After the Auxiliaries came the Black and Tans. These men were of a quite different and lower type. They were recruited openly for "a rough and dangerous task". While some were ex-soldiers, many were old jail birds, and men of disreputable character, and they came over to do dirty work in Ireland not with any patriotic motives, but for the high pay they were promised, and for the loot they hoped to get.

They were landed at the North Wall in batches of about 200 at a time, and they were marched by way of the quays to the depot in Phoenix Park. Their hardened, ruffianly faces created a very bad impression, and they lived up to it.

They were nicknamed the *"Black and Tans"* on account of the mixed colours of their uniforms. Those who were ex-soldiers wore their old khaki trousers, with a black civilian coat, and a policeman's cap and belt. Others were clothed in black trousers and khaki tunic.

This strange mixture and irregularity of attire, the result of the hurry in putting them in the field before RIC uniforms could be supplied to them, seemed to add to their already sinister appearance. Anyone who went through the fight will never forget the appearance of those villainous-looking fellows, dashing in their lorries through the streets, with their rifles or revolvers presented at the passers-by. They seemed deliberately to wear threatening and murderous expressions in order to terrorize the people. They took a prominent part in the raids, and were quite indifferent to the feelings of the women and children into whose houses they burst with murderous intent. But while they were able to cause misery and dismay there was no panic, and our resistance went on.

It was by these Auxiliaries and Black and Tans that the raid on 5 Mespil Road had been carried out, and their main object in raiding was to find and shoot Michael Collins. But, in fact, the tension was now so great, and the fear and the vindictiveness of the raiders so strong, that any man found with a gun on him had a very poor chance. In the areas in which Martial Law had been declared, a man found armed was punished with death. A number of our men had already been hanged. And even outside the Martial Law areas there was always the chance that a man found in a raided house would be shot. Excuses could be made. He had "fired on the raiding party" who "acted in self-defence", or he was "shot while trying to escape".

I had begun, therefore, besides the secret cupboards for documents, to construct hidden sleeping apartments in houses frequented by men 'on the run'. Merely to have a secret hole to creep into was of very little use. There was the warm vacated bed to give the show away, and the chance of some article of clothing left behind. The raiders did not wait long for a door to be opened. At the slightest delay, they would break it down with the butt ends of their rifles, and rush into the house.

Austin Stack had a very narrow escape in this way. He was staying in the house of Mrs. Gordon, and when the military thundered at the door, he jumped out of bed and hurried into his clothes. In his haste, he left one of his long golfing or bicycling stockings behind him. He climbed into a hidden recess which I had built over the trap door of the bath-room, but in crawling along, his foot came through the ceiling, knocking down a little of the plaster. The raiders walked over this fallen piece of plaster, but fortunately it did not occur to them to connect it with the movements of a man above. That was before the recruiting of the Black and Tans, and the British Military who conducted the raid were altogether a milder and less efficient set of men. Immediately Austin had left the bed, one of the girls from an adjoining room had got into it.

It was this incident which gave me the idea of constructing hidden sleeping apartments. For this a certain type of house was necessary—one in which a room could be cut off completely without it being apparent that a room was missing. To conceal the entrance to the room, I built in one of the usual wardrobes found so often in houses as permanent fixtures.

Such a hiding-place I constructed in the house of Mrs. Humphrey in the Ailesbury Road. The house was raided, but the room was not discovered, though the raiders searched with great thoroughness, and with their powerful electric torches closely examined every spot, including the wardrobe. All through the raid there were men in bed in the secret room, with only the thickness of the wardrobe wall between them and almost certain death— either at once, or later at the end of a rope in Mountjoy Jail.

I put these hiding-places to a severe test on one occasion. A brother of mine came up from Limerick on a visit to Dublin. He was also in the building trade and had thorough experience in the construction of all types of houses. I took him out to the house in Wellington Road which we had purchased, and to which I have already referred, and in which I had fitted up a secret room. I told him that I wanted to see if he could find it, and telling him to wait in the hall while he counted fifty, I went upstairs, opened the recess, got inside, and pulled-to the secret door behind me.

Soon I could hear him moving about the house, and around the room outside my hiding-place. I could almost feel him groping about the walls, and

I listened to him opening the wardrobe door and examining its interior. Then his footsteps retreated, and after a while he shouted from the hall—the signal we had agreed upon if his search was unsuccessful.

I came out and went down to him.

>*"Now I am going to let you into the secret"*, I told him. *"Come upstairs with me again."*

When I showed him the hidden room and the simplicity of its arrangement, he raised his hands in dismay.

>*"Ah, man dear"*, he said to me, *"that will never do at all! They will find it at once. For God's sake never put anyone you value in there. It is too simple".*

CHAPTER XXVII
A Rebuke From Michael Collins

The Mespil Road house is in my memory as the scene of many of my interviews with Michael Collins.

I have described an occasion when he praised me. There was another when he gave me a sharp rebuke. In business hours he was abrupt and stern in his manner. He had no patience for excuses for failure to carry out an order, and would waste no time listening to explanations.

We had run out of moulders sand and hard coke for one of our small bomb factories, and he sent for me and told me to procure a ton of this special coke.

I spent two days trying to get it, but discovered that it could only be sold to those carrying on a legitimate foundry trade. I had no means of proving that I was carrying on such a business.

I went to Michael and began explaining the situation to him but I had hardly uttered half a sentence before he snapped out, *"Have you got it, or have you not got it? If you haven't got it, don't mind the excuses, but go and get it"*.

I was standing beside his desk, and putting down his head he resumed his writing, with an air of dismissing me.

> *"Listen to me a moment, Michael. Though I have not been able to buy it, if you can wait till Saturday I can commandeer it".*
>
> *"That is all I want, Batt".* (He was now looking up at me again.) *"What are you wasting my time for? Go and commandeer it"*, he said impatiently.

Well, we commandeered it. He gave me the address to which it was to be taken, and I delivered the moulders sand myself. It was an old foundry in Crown Alley, close to Dublin Castle, the business of which was still being carried on in front. Our workshop was at the back, from which there was no exit, so that in the event of a raid it was a death-trap.

On giving the signal—two long knocks followed by two short ones—-the door was opened by a man I knew, Joe Furlong, who afterwards held the rank of Colonel in the National Army. Recognizing me, he said, *"Come in, Batt"*.

Within, there was a number of our men who were all stripped to the waist, casting bombs. Each had a loaded revolver beside him on his bench. Seeing them, I realized to the full the terrible risks our brave lads were running.

But with all Michael Collins's superficial sternness, he was of a tender and generous nature. He found time to help all who were in trouble or affliction. He was very thoughtful of the prisoners. He found means to get letters of encouragement and other more material consolations smuggled into them. How he accomplished such things, and got warders and wardresses in helping him to risk not only their livelihood, but their freedom, was another proof of his power which made him rise to such a height in our regard. Although it was so dangerous for him to go near the homes of those who were engaged actively in the fight, he never failed to do so if a visit from him would give support or consolation. He went to see Mrs. McKee after the tragic and terrible death of her splendid son in Dublin Castle.

He went out regularly to Greystones to see Mrs. de Valera and her children during the President's absence in America, and never failed to send him news of them in his official letters. He, himself, made all the arrangements for Mrs. de Valera's secret visit to the United States to join her husband, arranged for a lady friend to travel with her, saw to procuring passports for them under other names, and secured their tickets.

CHAPTER XXVIII
The Terror At Its Height

It was in Mespil Road, when I called one day, that Michael gave me these instructions:

> *"I have a job for you Batt. We have discovered that a number of their Secret Service men are living in private families all over the city. Some of them are in your respectable neighbourhood—Pembroke and Ballsbridge. I want you to get into touch with any postmen you can trust, and get them to hold up all letters directed to certain addresses which I will give you. They are probably getting their letters addressed under cover to the lady of the house".*

He then gave me a list, and I set to work to carry out his orders.

All letters for the Pembroke area are sorted at Ballsbridge Post Office. I happened to know a reliable man in the sorting office. He was an old Volunteer, and we had made acquaintance when we were fellow-prisoners in Richmond Barracks after the Rising.

I gave him the list of suspected houses, and not only did he agree at once to do what I wanted, but he offered to hold up all letters addressed to the officers of the Black and Tans at Beggar's Bush Barracks, which were also in the Ballsbridge postal district.

He got the postmen to help, so that soon we had a complete network of friendly postmen who handed over to me all letters directed to suspected houses according as we gave them notice of them.

The letters were brought to me to Brendan Road every night by my friend, the Volunteer. Sometimes there would be only a few, but occasionally he handed me as many as a couple of dozen. I hid them under the stair carpet, scattered over several steps, and evenly distributed so as not to appear bulky and cause suspicion. I did this in case of a raid. The next morning when I came home, as I often did to breakfast while I was on the run, I took them out and concealing them among my clothes I brought them to Mespil Road.

By means of these letters, and those which were held up in other districts in the same way, he gradually traced many of the British Secret Service agents and forestalled them.

He had continually to meet people who were in a position to give him information—either from our own ranks, or men employed in the offices of our opponents. This involved taking great risks. Some of those who came pretending to offer help were really agents of the British who were being used to bring about his destruction.

Two such men he met at my house. They were —— Jameson and Fergus Brian Molloy. He discovered that they were Secret Service men in the pay of the English.

Jameson had come over from England. His real name was Burn. He had approached Art O'Brien, our Sinn Féin representative in London, posing as a Bolshevist agent, and offering to smuggle in arms. So he came over with a letter of recommendation to Michael Collins, and actually handed over a few revolvers to show his good faith. He operated direct from Scotland Yard, and, strange to say, it was by one of the Dublin Castle G. men that he was given away. On hearing from Jameson that he had seen Michael Collins (at my house in Brendan Road), a detective named Redmond, of whom I shall have more to say, could not resist the impulse to taunt the other Castle agents with the fact. One of the G. men who was friendly to us heard Redmond exclaim: *"You are a bright lot! Not one of you has been able to get on to Collins's track for months, and here is a man only two days in Dublin who has already seen him."*

This gibe was reported to Michael Collins, and Jameson was at once suspected of being the man referred to. To make sure, he was allowed to see a portion of a letter, supposed to be from Michael Collins, in which he referred to important papers of his being in a certain place at a house, No. 9 Iona Drive. It was the residence of an ex-Lord Mayor, Mr. Farrell, who had received the King of England on one of his visits to Dublin. That night the house was raided, and it was ransacked for the documents which were supposed to be there, to the utter disgust of the gentleman of the house, who, shivering in his night attire, kept protesting: *"You are raiding your friends. Do you know that I received the King? I had twenty minutes conversation with him"*.

Jameson was found shot dead, soon afterwards, on the Ballymun Road.

Fergus Brian Mulloy came from the west of Ireland, highly recommended by Dr. Ferran, TD. He said he was an Army Sergeant, and was prepared to do dangerous work.

An appointment was made at my house. Michael told me to have a good supper, as he was bringing a military man that night who was going to be of great assistance to us in procuring arms.

In due time he arrived, accompanied by Liam Tobin, Assistant Director of Intelligence.

My wife, on going to open the door, got a set-back to see a man in British uniform; but recognizing Tobin she was reassured.

He came in and sat down by the fire beside me, to await the arrival of Michael Collins. I spoke to him of my surprise that a man wearing his uniform should come over to our side.

> *"Don't mind my uniform"*, he said: *"what you must take into account is my blood. I am the son of a Co. Mayo man who was forced to emigrate to England. Ever since your fight in 1916 the call of the blood has been urging me to assist the land of my father, and that is why I am taking such risks to help you".*

"All the same, it is strange to me to find a man with a purely English accent in our ranks".

> *"No matter about my accent"*, he replied. *"Am I not planning to hand you out a lot of guns from Wellington Barracks?"*

Then Michael arrived, and, after supper, I left the room to take my turn in keeping a look-out for a surprise raid.

His guilt was soon established, when he paid the penalty of his treachery.

Another man who had set out to betray Michael Collins was Quinlisk. He had been a prisoner of war in a German Internment Camp and was released to join Casement's brigade. Michael Collins had helped him financially, and had tried to get him employment. Later he fell under suspicion and a trap was laid for him. He was told *"confidentially"* that Michael Collins had gone down to Cork and would be there for several days. Immediately Quinlisk took train for Cork and began trying to locate him. The Cork men were waiting for him and brought his activities abruptly to an end. Quinlisk was the first spy shot by us.

Redmond, already referred to, was a very able Belfast man whom the English made use of in their efforts to remove Michael Collins. He was a clever detective and he brought six picked men with him from Belfast, and was appointed Assistant-Commissioner of the Dublin Force.

With the help of Jameson, Redmond discovered that Michael Collins dined nearly every day at 1 Brendan Road. James MacNamara, of the Dublin Detective Division, got hold of this information and passed it on to Michael. The next day, at the hour when he should have been there, the house was raided. Anticipating the raid, Michael Collins had bicycled along the Morehampton Road (out of which Brendan Road diverges), and he soon detected the 'spotter' who was waiting about to give the word that he had arrived. Michael passed close to him on his bicycle, and then turned round into Brendan Road, riding swiftly past the house, and out of sight past the corner of the next street.

When the spotter reached the corner of Brendan Road there was no sign of Michael Collins. Obviously, he was in No. 1. He was caught at last! He gave the glad tidings to Redmond and his party, who arrived in several armoured cars a few minutes afterwards. The house was surrounded and searched. But Michael Collins was not there! He had gone straight to the home of Fionán Lynch, in Pembroke Road. There, too, was Gearóid O'Sullivan, and the three of them waited for the news of the raid which would be brought to them by Joe O'Reilly.

After that we saw to it that Redmond troubled us no more.

Our Intelligence was so good, and punishment so swift, that it became more and more difficult to get Irishmen to act as spies. The English then tried sending over a number of officers from their own Secret Service Branch in London. These men, too, were, one by one, traced by Michael Collins and the men of his Intelligence Department, and sixteen of them were shot on the morning of the 21st November 1920.

They had been too careful to take up their residence in Dublin Castle, where they would either have had to remain as prisoners within its walls, or to become marked men by our 'spotters' who watched everyone who came out of it. So they took lodgings in private families, and a number of them rented all the service flats in a house in Pembroke Street. Here they lived in great privacy. They dressed as civilians, adopted assumed names, and never left the house until after Curfew, when they took part in midnight raids, in which a number of Volunteers and civilians were shot out of hand before they had time to get out of their beds. They collected their information by means of touts, and kept written records of the result of their activities. Some of these records fell into our hands after the shootings, and gave ample proof that the lives of our men depended upon our striking first.

The British took immediate reprisals. On the same afternoon there was a football match at Croke Park, and the place was surrounded, when British soldiers fired warning upon the crowd. Fourteen people were killed and over fifty wounded. They were mainly country people who had come up to see the match, and were taking no part in the fight.

On the previous night, Dick McKee, Peadar Clancy, and Conor Clune had been arrested and taken to Dublin Castle. After the shootings they were killed in the Castle, and their bodies were ultimately given to their relatives for burial. A story was given out that, while prisoners, they had seized arms which were lying about, and had attacked their Guard. But there was no real secret made of the fact that they had been killed deliberately and their terribly mutilated bodies told their own story.

At great personal risk Michael Collins attended the Requiem Mass, and I was one of the two men who walked beside the hearse to Glasnevin. The other was Michael O'Neill, a returned Clan na Gael man from San Francisco. The raiding was now ceaseless, and as the funeral emerged out of O'Connell

Street, it was found that the British Military had invested the east side of Parnell Square. It had, therefore, to be diverted to Parnell Street, and the west side of the Square.

I knew Michael would want to hear about the funeral and on my return I went to Mespil Road.

I found him feeling very sadly over the loss of our two great soldiers, McKee and Clancy. He paid a very high tribute to Dick McKee. He talked much more freely than usual, so moved he was, and I noticed it the more because he so seldom praised anyone. So much so, that the names of the few men and women he did praise are in my memory as surely the best of all the good people we had in those years. Speaking that day, in great sorrow, of the loss of Dick McKee, he said:

> *"It will be almost impossible to find a man to fill his place. There was no one like him for the thoroughness with which he made all the arrangements for carrying out a difficult or dangerous undertaking. He never overlooked the smallest detail. And you know, Batt, in our fight, to fail to foresee everything, and arrange for everything, means disaster. I always consulted him on my own plans before I put them into execution. He was my right-hand man in arranging all the details for the escape of our men from the prisons. I would first submit to him my arrangements for any action I proposed to take, and if they stood the test of Dick's approval in every particular, then and then only would I go on with the work".*

He concluded with these words: *"Such was the great soldier you have laid to rest to-day, and who had so small a funeral".*

From that day the fight had an added grimness. All our leading men and our Intelligence officers and our best soldiers had known that if they fell into the hands of their enemies they would be shot or hanged. That possibility—that probability—had been faced by them. But they had hoped for a clean and humane end, if it came. But after the cruel death suffered by Dick McKee and the two others who were with him, only one hope was left. They determined, each one of them, not to be taken alive, but to die fighting.

For those of us who knew and loved Michael Collins the days and weeks which followed were a period of the most painful anxiety. Every night upon my knees I prayed to Almighty God to protect him, not only for the great love I had for him, but because I knew that if we lost him all our efforts were in vain. Every day and every night hundreds of trained men were hunting for him. Who but Almighty God could save him? If I had not had faith in prayer and the goodness of God, during those last months of the struggle I would have given way to despair.

CHAPTER XXIX
Increasing Tension And A Merry Christmas!

But though he must have felt the strain he gave no sign of it.

I met him one day in this same month of November 1920, when the English had already put a price of £10,000 on his head. He was walking along a thickly-populated street in the City swinging a folded newspaper in his hand. He was as cool and innocent looking as any other passer-by. He counted upon the fact (and was justified) that the enemy would not give him credit for such daring, for such a power of self-control.

He stopped and greeted me.

"Where is the old bike", I asked him.

"It is not necessary for the errand on which I am engaged this morning, Batt. I am going to meet an Archbishop."

He was on his way to keep an appointment with Archbishop Clune who had been sent over as an intermediary to see whether a truce were possible. There is no need to repeat here how those hopes of peace were frustrated at that time by the too precipitate action of the Rev. Fr. O'Flanagan, and the Galway County Council. But since I have mentioned that fact, it is only fair to add that the English, in their public utterances and through their private emissaries, made a condition then which could not have been accepted by us. Before there could be any talk of peace, they said, three of our men who "were reasonably suspected of having committed murder" must first be given up. It was obvious who the three men were: Michael Collins, Richard Mulcahy, Chief of Staff and Cathal Brugha, Minister of Defence. These were the men against whom the murder campaign of the English was mainly directed.

After we lost the house in Mespil Road I bought another for Michael Collins in Harcourt Terrace.

The owner of the house was a Jew, and I got a woman I knew to come along with me to be the intended purchaser. I drove a very hard bargain with the Jewish gentleman, and I think he admired my business abilities. I told him that the lady was a cousin of mine, and that I was naturally anxious to make a good deal for her.

He was a decent, honest man. I met him after the Truce when he had learned that the house he sold "my cousin" had been used as an office by Michael Collins. *"Ah! If I had only known!"* he exclaimed. *"I used to wonder at all the young men going in and out of the place, and the lady not coming near it at all! If I had only known it was used by Michael Collins! Sure, I would have stayed up, myself, all night to mind him"*. He then gave me a generous subscription for our funds.

It was only a month or so after 5 Mespil Road was discovered that the Mary Street office was raided. They missed Michael Collins that morning by only a minute or two. He had just left the building, and must have been still in the street when the raiders rushed in.

That raid upset him greatly. It was the first time I ever saw him seriously troubled.

"*Batt*", he said, "*they will get me now in a fortnight*".

I was completely taken aback to hear him speak so, such a change it was from his usual self-confident manner.

"*Arrah! Michael, not at all! Sure isn't Almighty God protecting you*".

"*Ah! it is different this time, Batt*", he said, with emotion. "*I am being given away from inside, and those who knew about Mary Street know everything else about me.*"

Greatly troubled to hear him, I tried to turn his mind away from this idea by speaking of another house to take the place of the office he had lost, but he interrupted me.

"*No*", he said, "*I won't go there. I am coming back to work in my old quarters in Brendan Road.*"

"*Good God! Are you mad? It was yourself who forbade me to sleep at home. Are you forgetting that the house has been raided over and over again?*"

"*That is the very reason why I am coming back to it! It has been raided so often that it is the last house they will expect to find me in. And I can trust those who are inside it. I shall know where I am.*"

So he came back again to my house in Brendan Road, and worked there until the Truce.

While the Terror was at its height, on Christmas night, 1920, in the midst of all our anxieties, I spent two most enjoyable hours. Michael Collins with Tom Cullen, one of his chief Intelligence Officers, and Gearóid O'Sullivan, and Joe O'Reilly called out to my house at about eight o'clock to wish me a happy Christmas.

We were all in good spirits, feeling the presence of the festive season in spite of the danger and stress surrounding us. While we were talking and having a drink, Michael casually said: "*It is little short of a miracle that we are all here to-night*".

"*Why so?*" said I.

"*Because this time last night five of us were in the Gresham Hotel surrounded by fourteen Auxiliaries all pointing their revolvers at us.*"

"*My God, what happened?*"

"Besides Tom, Liam, and Gearóid we had Rory O'Connor with us. I was standing a dinner on account of a bet I had won off them. We were in a private room when a waiter ran in to tell us that the hotel was raided, and we had only time to push any scraps of paper we had on us into our socks before the door burst open.

"Of course we were not armed. There was a crowd of them, and we were immediately surrounded and held up."

" 'Stand up", I was commanded.

" 'What is your name?"

" 'John Grace," I replied.

" 'What is your job? Where do you work?"

" 'I am an accountant. My office is in Dame Street."

"On a loose-leaf ledger in my pocket I had pencilled the word "rifles", to remind me of something. I swore it was not "rifles" but 'refills'.*

"The others also made up good names and occupations, and plausible explanations of their presence.

"They were very suspicious of me. I was questioned over and over again. One Officer actually drew that old photograph of me out of his pocket, and compared it with my face, drawing my hair down as it was in the picture. It was touch and go. They were not quite satisfied, and hesitated long before they left us; but here we are to have one more merry Christmas, anyway."

I nearly dropped to hear of this narrow escape of almost the whole of the Headquarters' Intelligence Staff, and our most indispensable men, but Michael's gaiety and coolness soon helped me to recover.

I suggested that we should send round for Liam Mellowes and Seán Etchingham, whose house of shelter was close by, and make the most of the short time left before Curfew.

Everyone was willing, and they were with us in a few minutes, when we gave ourselves up to hilarity. I made some excellent punch, and each of us gave a song or a recitation. When it came to Mellowes' turn he said he was no singer, but he would give us some imitations of speeches he had heard in America. He first imitated de Valera, whom he called *"The Professor"*, then Judge Cohalan, and Dr. Pat McCartan. He had us in roars of laughter, and it came as a shock when somebody, who had the presence of mind to look at his watch, announced: *"It is ten o'clock. Time's up".*

We all scattered immediately to our respective dug-outs.

Joe O'Reilly told me afterwards how he and Tom Cullen got home. Fortified with my punch, they ran by back lanes all the way to Westland Row where they picked up a hack. Tumbling into the cab, they told the jarvey to drive them to Devlin's, that house of unfailing hospitality. Defying Curfew, the enemy, and all his works, they sang songs, till they reached Parnell Street, but when they began to knock at the door at nearly eleven o'clock at night, they roused the darkest suspicions in the breasts of those who were within. The whole of the empty street echoed with their hammering, and it was only when they were on the verge of desperation, with the sound of an approaching military lorry, that they gained admission. Liam Tobin and others of our men were inside, and naturally took the visitors coming at such an hour for enemy raiders. They were halfway out of the back windows ready for an attempted escape, after sending down a young lad employed in the house to open the door. There was a very hearty interchange of language between the besiegers and the besieged—each cursing the others for the frights they had suffered.

CHAPTER XXX

The Truce

In May and June 1921 ammunition for the men on active service had all but run out. It was almost impossible to secure supplies. Many of the sources through which they were smuggled in had had to be abandoned, as the watching and searching at every port and harbour had become very keen and efficient. There was no procuring arms except those which could be captured after an ambush or during an attack. During the many investments of one after another area of the City many of our dumps had necessarily been discovered. From all our fighting centres came urgent appeals for ammunition, and about the middle of May the officers of a Southern Command, one of whom was Liam Lynch, (afterwards a leader in the Civil War on the anti-Treaty side), reported to Michael Collins that without fresh supplies they could not carry on much longer.

Early in June, therefore, it was with a feeling of immense relief that we heard that the English were making fresh moves for an armistice. General Smuts had been encouraged to take a hand in outlining a basis upon which terms of peace might be discussed, and rumours were about of an offer of Dominion Home Rule.

Then two things happened which went to strengthen our hopes. In opening the Belfast Parliament on the 23rd June King George made a speech of conciliation, and on the same day de Valera, after having been arrested in a house in Blackrock, was immediately released.

I have seen a letter, captured in the post, from the officer who arrested de Valera. It was written to a friend, a fellow officer in England. Describing the incident he said that he had had the pleasure of causing a sensation by arresting de Valera on the day the King went to open the Northern Parliament. He did not know the identity of his prisoner till he had taken him to Dublin Castle. Strange to say, he wrote, he did not seem quite pleased to be set free.

We were not altogether unprepared, therefore, when coming at last into the open, Lloyd George sent his letter to the press inviting Sinn Féin to appoint representatives with authority to discuss terms of peace.

Everyone was overjoyed. To get even a respite from the strain which had been growing almost intolerable gave extreme satisfaction. Everybody I met was enthusiastic over the prospect of the war being over, and the feeling of the general public can be gauged when it is remembered that the crowd loudly cheered General MacCready when he passed through Dawson Street on his way to the Mansion House to arrange the terms of the Truce. The women, especially, prayed aloud that God would aid their efforts for peace.

Michael Collins was disturbed by this excess of enthusiasm, or at least by the public expression of it, before the Truce was an accomplished fact. *"It will give the impression that we are only too willing to give in"*, he said.

A few days afterwards, Con Collins called to Brendan Road. We were joined there by Michael Collins, and the three of us went together to the house of a friend of mine to have a drink and talk over the Truce. As we were sitting in the private bar, the proprietor, hearing I was in the place, came in to see me. I whispered to Michael: *"He has been a good friend; may I tell him who you are?"*

"All right, Batt", he replied: *"go ahead"*.

At first the good man could not believe my words.

"What! Michael Collins! Is this really Michael Collins!" he kept repeating, his face suffused with emotion, and when Michael shook his hand, his joy and pride were unbounded. He rushed out of the room and was back again in a moment with a bottle of liqueur whisky, the best in his cellar, he told us. He begged us to honour him by being his guests.

Michael, who was delighted with his simplicity and good nature, was sitting on a table in the middle of the room. He was swinging his legs in a way he had, and immediately above his head was a small electric bell hanging from the ceiling by a cord. Every time he moved, his head touched the bell-push, and every time it was touched it rang outside in the public bar and a barman appeared in answer to it; and each time the barman appeared our host waved his arms at him, shouting with great impatience, *"Go away! we don't want you. What are you pushing in here for?"*—so fearful he was of missing a word spoken by Michael, or of being distracted for a moment from drinking in the fact of his presence.

A year afterwards when Michael was killed, that sincere, simple man cut off the little bell-push, and put it away in a place of safety. On rare occasions, he will take it out to show it to one whom he thinks worthy of so great a privilege.

"Do you see that?" he will say. *"That little bell-push is my greatest treasure.* **It touched the head of Michael Collins"**.

We did not stay long and went back to my house.

Well, the drink had been good, and we were lighthearted, and, guessing we needed it, my wife made haste to prepare us some supper. She brought in a large dish of sausages and fried eggs, and soon the three of us were seated round the table.

Michael was in a mischievous mood. He began to taunt Con, poking fun at him, half in jest and half in earnest, and as he continued his banter Con would look away. And every time his eyes left his plate for a moment, Michael with his fork stole one of his sausages! Looking at his plate again, Con stared at it with a puzzled gaze, and took a bite of what was left with an expression which said: *"I dare say it is only my fancy, but I do not remember eating that last one"*.

My wife was in the room looking on at us.

"Won't you stay here to-night, Michael", she said, *"now that it is safe for you?"*

"I will not, Mrs. O'Connor", he replied: *"you have done enough for us all for the present. I am going back to my old lodgings in Mountjoy Street, and don't you put up anyone. Let them go to their hotels. I don't know how long the Truce will last, and we may want you again."*

Turning to me, he said: *"Batt, I have no doubt there will be many houses open to me now, but when I was hard pressed there were not more than five upon which I could count for a genuine welcome"*.

CHAPTER XXXI
Memorable Meetings With Michael Collins.
The Treaty Of Peace

Two later meetings with Michael Collins stand out in my memory. Perhaps because on both occasions he was in deep distress, and in my more familiar pictures I see him gay, laughing, self-reliant, sometimes stern and angry, but rarely downcast.

He came to see me on the day in September 1921 when he had been selected as one of the five plenipotentiaries to go to London to discuss terms of peace.

He was greatly upset. He would not sit down, but kept pacing the floor, his face set in lines of pain and anxiety.

"I should not have been asked to go", he said. *"I pleaded strongly against my selection."*

"But, Michael", I urged, *"you are our big man. You will win better terms for us than anyone else."*

"It is a mistake to send me. De Valera should go. Who ever heard of the soldier who fought the enemy in the field being sent to negotiate the peace?" he cried. *"I am being put in an impossible position."*

"Sit down, man, and let us talk about it".

He did not seem to hear me; but continued to stride up and down the floor.

"I fought hard against my selection", he burst out again. *"De Valera pressed me. For no other man living would I have consented."*

The English had made use of his name in their propaganda as their most extreme and irreconcilable enemy in Ireland, he said. Wise counsels would take advantage of that fact. He should have been allowed to remain a hidden force behind the scenes, and his name used during the negotiations to extract the maximum terms from the other side. That was his argument.

"Peace must mean of necessity some adjustment of the extreme demands on both sides—on ours as well as theirs. It is not the soldiers who fought on either side who should settle that adjustment. Who is to direct the fight if we have to go back to war, which is only too likely?"

But he did not shirk the odious duty, the one most uncongenial to him of all the services he rendered his country.

He came back to Dublin on the 8th December with the Treaty, having fought the English as hard over the Conference table as ever he did in the field. He and his colleagues won for their country in two months a measure of Independence beyond the most sanguine hopes of the Fenians, and far in excess of the demands made by Parnell.

They secured the recognition of Dáil Eireann as the *de jure* Parliament in Dublin; the IRA as the nucleus of a National Army, and complete fiscal freedom and the control of our own finances, a right which Erskine Childers had sought in vain to have recognized in the Home Rule Act of 1914. The terms of the Treaty in regard to North-East Ulster were such, that, while the six counties were not to be forced to come under the Dublin Parliament against their will, if we had remained united in the twenty-six counties behind the Treaty, and had not, by fighting amongst ourselves, seemed to show that we were unfit for self-government, the unity of Ireland in a short period was assured. It was in that belief that the clauses relating to North-East Ulster were agreed to by Michael Collins.

But de Valera refused to stand by the colleague who had undertaken, at his own urgent plea, the task which he himself had refused, and who had certainly "done his best for Ireland in the circumstances" which arose.

It was late at night when I saw him on that day of his return home. I had read the Treaty terms in the newspaper that morning with profound thankfulness, both for what they gave in fact, and for what they held in promise for the future.

There was a knock at the door. I opened it myself. Michael Collins was on the doorstep. He did not walk in, but remained standing, looking at me with a strange expression.

"Come in. What are you waiting for? Ah, Michael! This is a day I never thought I would live to see."

"I thought perhaps you would have no welcome for me, Batt", he said.

Coming in, he told me at once, that de Valera was going to repudiate the Treaty.

It is hard to describe his frame of mind. He was beside himself. Now at last I saw shaken to his depths that strong man on whom we had all leaned. He doubted his power to carry the Treaty against the opposition of de Valera. He saw the Truce at an end, with no hope of a successful issue a second time. After the long truce the *morale* of the men was not what it was. Discipline had been relaxed. Everything was now known. Our men had appeared publicly. It was known where were all our secret meeting places. It would be impossible to carry on, on the old lines.

"I will leave Dublin at once", he said, in a tone of extreme bitterness and distress. *"I will go down to Cork. If the fighting is going to be resumed, I will fight in the open, beside my own people down there. I am not going to be chivvied and hunted through Dublin as I have been for the last two years."*

I argued with him:

"If we go back to the fight, how long could we stick it?
"A fortnight, and it would all be over."
"Without you in Dublin, who would there be to lead us?"
"There is a coming man. He will take my place".
"Whom do you mean?"
"I mean Eoin O'Duffy." (Now Commissioner of the Civic Guard.)

I appealed to him not to desert the people who looked to him as their leader and saviour.

"Michael", I said, *"I have never praised you. You would not have cared for that. But now I am going to tell you that you are such a man as we never had before in Ireland, so that we have grown to look to you to do what no one else can do for us. Do not fail us. You have brought back this Treaty. It is a wonderful achievement. The people want it. They must at least be given the chance to say what they think of it. Then if they reject it, (only they will not reject it), you will have done your part, and will have no responsibility for the consequences."*

This appeal to stand by the people had an immediate effect on him.

He had been, as on that former occasion, striding up and down the room, flinging out his arms, speaking words betraying passionate emotion. But now he grew calm, and sat down beside me at last. He did not leave till three o'clock in the morning. Before we parted he assured me that he would not leave Dublin. He would see the Treaty through the Dáil, and would see that its terms were fully discussed and put clearly before the people.

"I will accept their verdict", he said.

I kept in touch.with him through the debates in the Dáil. I told him of what I had learned, that his opponents were canvassing extensively in the country, and that pressure was being brought to bear even on the Volunteers (the IRA).

He replied that he was well aware of the truth of what I said, but that so far as he was concerned he would try to influence nobody. He would do no canvassing, and would allow none of his supporters to approach the Army and try to win it for the Treaty. He would defend it in the Dáil, explain its provisions, and his reason for accepting it. After that, the people could take it or leave it.

He kept his word, and perhaps he was right. But it may be also that his defensive attitude was misunderstood in the country. There is no doubt that numbers were opposed to the Treaty through ignorance of the full significance of its terms. It was so easy to misrepresent it to simple, uncritical minds. In his speech in the Dáil, Michael Collins said: *"I do not claim that the Treaty gives us the full freedom which all nations aspire to, but I claim that it gives us freedom to achieve that end".* If the full import of that sentence had been understood and accepted, no true patriot, whatever actual form of government he might favour, could have opposed it or voted against it.

By making a Truce with us, and by the terms of that Truce, our claim to be a nation with the right to use military means to secure our national independence had been at last recognized by the British. That was the first and the most important proof of the change in the relationship of the two countries brought about by the 1916-21 struggle. There could be no going back from that recognition, and the Treaty terms were the legal expression of it. Those who belittled the terms of the Treaty were in fact belittling the strength of the position we won by the success of the five years' struggle. The Treaty was made with the Irish people as the people of a belligerent nation, and Ireland's status rests upon the Treaty on that basis, and not on any English statutory reform like Home Rule. It was made with *the whole Irish nation* through its acknowledged plenipotentiaries who had carried on the war. It contained only an option for North-East Ulster. We had always been ready to settle with our North-Eastern population by conference and agreement. If there had been no Civil War, and Michael Collins and Arthur Griffith had survived, the prestige of the Irish Nation at its height would have led to a suitable national settlement.

The Treaty was ratified. But it was ratified only by a majority of seven. If there had been a more decisive verdict our subsequent history would certainly have been different. The opponents of the Treaty took heart from the smallness of the majority, a totally inadequate one as expressing the opinions of the people, who were not consulted. If their wishes had been ascertained and their true verdict on the Treaty expressed by an ample majority in the Dáil, there is little doubt that there would have been no Civil War, and consequently no Boundary.

Had the opponents of the Treaty relied upon *"a constitutional way of settling our differences"* (de Valera), opposition and fair criticism in the Dáil would have not weakened but strengthened our power to use the Treaty for the fulfilment of those national aspirations upon the promotion of which we had hitherto all been united. It was not the wish of Michael Collins to see all the Irish people, through their representatives, supporting the Treaty as the last word in Irish Independence. A left wing in the Dáil, in constitutional opposition, would have strengthened his hands.

CHAPTER XXXII
The Surrender Of Dublin Castle

One event shall ever abide in my memory as giving me the proudest moment of my life.

It was the day, the 16th January 1922, when I stood in Dublin Castle Yard waiting for the arrival of Michael Collins to take over the evacuated Castle from the English.

It seemed to be fitting that it was into the hands of young Michael Collins that it should be surrendered. He was one of the people, of pure Irish stock, coming from a family who had been settled on the soil of Ireland for centuries. And it was he, by the power of his genius and character, and the strength of his patriotism, who had at last brought about that surrender.

As I waited I thought how, only twelve months before, raiding parties from this very Castle were rushing out, day and night, to hunt for him. And now I was to behold him arrive to take over this British stronghold, which for more than seven centuries had been the military headquarters of the invaders, and from which my beloved country had been so cruelly governed. Tears of joy rolled down my cheeks and my heart was fit to burst with pride and gratitude.

Michael had been in the country for the week-end, and had missed the early train to Dublin, so that he arrived twenty minutes later than the hour fixed for the historic ceremony.

The streets were filled with dense crowds. While we waited, I overheard a conversation between two English officers in mufti.

"Our flag has been hauled down this morning", said one of them, *"but you will see it back again before six months. Those fellows have begun already to fight among themselves. Well, I daresay I shall be back again then. I was here at Easter 1916, during their Rebellion. I was on the* **Helga** *which came up the Liffey, and bombarded Liberty Hall."*

"That's strange", said the other officer. *"I was here too. I rigged up a substitute for an armoured car with a boiler, and from it we peppered the rebels with machine-gun fire in the O'Connell Street area."*

At that moment I heard loud cheering along Dame Street. It came nearer and nearer till it was taken up by the crowd assembled in the Castle Yard.

A taxi appeared. Out of it jumped Michael Collins accompanied by Kevin O'Higgins, Fionán Lynch, and Eamonn Duggan. He ran lightly up the steps inside the Castle. Lord Fitzalan, the Viceroy, was waiting to receive him, and with him were other officials deeply imbued with the solemnity of the occasion.

"You are welcome, Mr. Collins", they said. Michael's smile, I heard, was a little grim.

It was all over in a few minutes.

On his way out he caught sight of me. He invited me into his car. The five of us drove to the Mansion House where Arthur Griffith was waiting.

Pushing open the door on the left of the entrance, he strode into the room, and announced:

"Griffith! The Castle has fallen."

CHAPTER XXXIII

The Death Of Michael Collins

On the 22nd August, 1922, Michael Collins was shot dead near Bandon, Co. Cork. The news of his death was broken to me at the dawn of morning on 23rd August by my two friends, Major General Tom Cullen and Colonel Joe O'Reilly.

The sad tidings had been sent by wireless to Portobello Barracks, and they came to my house, as day was breaking, to save me the terrible shock of reading the news in the morning paper.

I have the picture for ever in my mind of those two fearless men standing beside my bed, their eyes streaming with tears. They were both much younger men than I, yet they tried to support me, to help me to bear our common desolation. Telling me to brace myself for the news they had to tell, they said:.

"Mick was ambushed and killed in his own county last evening."

As soon as they could recover their voices to say a little more, they told me that his body was being brought to Dublin, and would lie in the mortuary of St. Vincent's Hospital, Stephen's Green.

Early on the following morning I was standing beside his bier, alone; gazing fondly with a breaking heart upon all that was left of the grandest character I have ever known.

I must draw a veil over the anguish of that morning.

**

If I were asked what I considered were the traits of character in Michael Collins which impressed me most, I would say, first, his amazing courage, and next, his close-mindedness.

There was something in his manner which gave him the power or charm of imbuing those in close touch with him with a share of both those qualities. One could not feel fear in his company. His coolness was infectious. If it were suggested to him that he should not do a certain thing because of its dangerous nature, he would unhesitatingly start to carry it out. I believe he did so, not from any spirit of bravado, but to give us some of his own supreme confidence; to prove to us that nothing was too dangerous to do, if it was done with coolness, self-control, and steady resolution.

Perhaps the most remarkable thing about him was what I have called his close-mindedness, and I mean by that his power to keep his own counsel. He had very little to say about the things that happened. Striking, dramatic things were happening every day planned by him, or staged by the enemy for his capture. Yet nobody had less to say about them than Michael Collins. There were no notes of exclamation. He referred to them, if at all, in a word or two. It was not that he was not stirred by the events of the living drama of which he was the chief actor and hero, but that he had schooled himself to a habit of silence upon which not only his own life and the lives of others depended, but the success of the struggle in which we were engaged.

But when he spoke, his words were plain, direct, and to the point. We could rely unquestioningly on their accuracy, whether he were describing something which had taken place, or were giving instructions how some action was to be carried out. Nothing could be more remote from the habit of mind of Michael Collins than to show any kind of brag or boasting in his speech. On the contrary, if he referred at all to what was being done and his own part in the fight, he did so with an air, as it were, of brushing it aside.

Yet all the time, without thinking about it, we knew that he was the life and soul of the struggle. We knew that without him our fight would have been the fight of a handful of untrained and practically unarmed men against the enormous army of a mighty Empire. It was his brain and character—his indomitable will, his unerring judgment, his courage, and his matchless energy—in a word, the splendid genius of one young Irishman—which wiped out our inequalities, gave us strength of spirit for strength of numbers, the weapons of superior resourcefulness to make good the deficiency in our arms.

It was not that he practised any false modesty. He was too honest for that. He did not undervalue what was being done any more than he overvalued it. But it was not the time for gloating; nor for regretting. There was no time to weep, and the time had not yet come to rejoice. "Get on with the work", was his watchword.

Unconsciously, we modelled ourselves upon him. At least, so far as our lesser natures would allow. It was a proof of our admiration; one of the ways in which we expressed our worship of him. So there was very little loose talk. We got on with the work.

CHAPTER XXXIV

The End Of My Story

From 1919 to the date of the ratification of the Treaty, I was Chairman of the *Comhairle Ceanntar* of Sinn Féin for the Pembroke constituency. I was also Treasurer of the O'Rahilly Sinn Féin Club for the same period. When the new organization, Cumann na nGaedheal, was set up to take the place of the Sinn Féin organization I was elected to the Standing Committee as Joint Treasurer, a position I still hold. In 1923, I was appointed a Peace Commissioner for the City and County of Dublin.

In March 1924 I was selected as the Cumann na nGaedheal (Government) candidate to contest the seat in Co. Dublin made vacant by the death of M.J. Derham. My anti-Treaty opponent was my old friend Seán MacEntee.

At that time the Cumann na nGaedheal organization was by no means the perfect election machine it is to-day, and mostly all the work of organizing the different areas of the county fell on my own shoulders. The work came easy to me, however, as I had had good training in electioneering ever since 1917. President Cosgrave, and the late Kevin O'Higgins, and other Ministers addressed meetings on my behalf.

The Election was hard fought, without any bitterness, so that I regretted that my opponent and old associate, Seán MacEntee, should have allowed a Belfast barrister to attack me about the gold which Michael Collins had entrusted to me. This barrister, who so far as I know never lost a night's sleep for the Cause, said in a speech: *"When Mr. O'Connor became the custodian of the gold he was only a working man, but now he is a prosperous employer. Collins is dead and where is the gold?"* A true Cause needs neither lies nor slander to support it, and I beat my opponent by two to one.

It is now June 1929, and I still sit for Co. Dublin in my native Parliament.

I have much to thank God for, and every day I praise His name for the glories I have been privileged to see. Words fail me to express the joy and pride I feel each morning when I see our Irish soldiers march past, with drums beating to the music of the Irish Pipes, to relieve the guard at the Bank of Ireland in College Green.

Never once have I seen them but I stand to admire them, remove my hat in respect, and breathe a prayer of thankfulness that I have lived to behold Ireland's first National Army since the days of Sarsfield. Often in the past, when I saw the Army of Occupation march through the streets of Dublin, in full equipment, and with disdain in their looks, did I wish and pray for the time to come when their presence and power would be unknown in our land. That time I never hoped to live to see; but it has come. Deep down in my heart I feel a wonderful gratitude that any effort of mine, however feeble, should have helped to hasten the glorious event. I like sometimes to fancy Tom Clarke and Seán MacDermott standing quietly beside me, unnoticed among the passers-by, watching our soldiers marching past in their green uniforms. To me such a sight never grows familiar, and I thank God who has spared me to witness it.

My little history is the story of the chief events in the life of a plain man to whom some privileges and honours and many blessings came, by the grace of God. I saw our national struggle, which had been carried on for centuries through darkness and despair, brought to a successful issue. I saw my countrymen rise to a height of greatness, courage, and devotion they had never reached before. I was the associate of noble men whose names will be honoured for ever in my country. But above all those privileges, for which I humbly thank God, there is one which stands above them all, the memory of which is the proudest possession of my life—my friendship with Michael Collins. If I were ever tempted to fall away from my idea of what a son of Ireland should be, there would rise before me the image of that glorious character, and what he would expect of me. There is my bulwark.

Solus na bhflaithis d'a' anam.

The light of heaven to his soul.

Statement Of Mrs. Batt O'Connor

1.   The full account of our early association with the national movement is in my husband's book. I had my domestic occupations of course, looking after my house and children and was not directly associated with any movement except the Gaelic League, which I joined shorty after I came to Dublin. My husband was already in it, being a member of the Keating Branch and I also became a member. We regularly attended the classes and other functions together.

2.   We all know that, as well as for the teaching of Irish, the Gaelic League was used for other purposes, especially political, and the volunteers were to a large extent recruited from its members and also the IRB. It was through that I got to know all the fighting men. Sean T. O'Kelly was, I think, President of the Branch at that time, and Fionan Lynch, Gearoid O'Sullivan, Piaras Beaslai, Diarmuid O'Hegarty and his brother were members too. These men were all visitors to my house before things assumed the serious aspect they afterwards did.

3.   After the inception of the Volunteers there were often very important meetings held at my house. During those visits on their business matters I naturally became acquainted with them and friendly with many of them.
      As the Volunteer movement developed and became serious, I became acquainted with dozens more. Coming on towards the fight numbers of men came to the house for meetings &c. Amongst them were Sean McDermott, Con Collins and Cathal Brugha. Charlie Monahan used to come. He was a great man in connection with arms and ammunition.

4.   In preparation for Easter Week a large quantity of arms and ammunition, mostly ammunition, was brought to our house at Brendan Road and hidden in a building plot at the end of the road. Two boxes of cartridges were brought to the house and the cartridges were hidden in every available spot including the hollow kerbs on the fireplaces. During the day preceding Easter Week the Volunteers came singly, in pairs and in groups, to fetch the cartridges and ammunition. Not all the ammunition in the building plot was removed before the Rising. On the Morning after the surrender the house was raided; it was raided many times after, but this was the worst raid we ever had. The military evidently expected to find men and arms, but they found

nothing. They were so disappointed at getting nothing in the house that they asked me to come down and show them what was down in the building yard. I walked them round the plot, actually over the places where the stuff was stored but they got nothing. The officer said *"I am sorry, Mrs. O'Connor, for this disturbance, but we must do our duty"*. I said *"it is all right, you got nothing anyway"*. I felt very much alone, with my five young children, having no sympathy from any side in Donnybrook except from the O'Rahilly's who lived in Herbert Park. My husband was away and I was uncertain of his fate. I felt great satisfaction in being able to say *"you got nothing"*. The officer was very polite and shook hands with me and apologised again before going away.

5.   I am recounting these facts which probably are not very important. But now in my old age I like to recall them. It gives me great solace to remember that I had the privilege of cooking, washing for and putting up all those great men who sacrificed themselves for Ireland and I would be very happy to do it all over again.

6.   One of these especially I was very glad to be able to help because he was suffering great pain. That was Sean McDermott. Some months before the Rising he got a breakdown and had to go into the Mater Hospital with neuritis in his leg. He almost lost the use of it. My husband brought him out to our house for Christmas—this must have been the Christmas before the Rising,—against the advice of the doctor. Sean took it on himself to leave the hospital because he was determined to be in the fight. He was five weeks with us and during these weeks there was not a day some of the leading men did not come to see him. It was then I met Thomas McDonagh, Major McBride and many others whom I did not meet again as they lost their lives in the fight.

7.   I was in great anxiety during and after Easter Week because I did not know where my husband was. I did not see or hear from him since he left home for Kerry on Good Friday.

9.   A message was brought to me a few days after the surrender by a released prisoner that my husband was detained in Richmond Barracks. The message—that I could come to see him—was written on the flap of an envelop in Batt's handwriting and signed by him. The messenger looked like a G-man and, therefore, I did not give him too friendly a reception. He was a traveller for a builders' providers firm and he understood my frame of mind.

He was very sympathetic and told me that my husband was in great form. I'll never forget the relief that was to me—to learn that he was alive.

9.   I went to see him the very next day. What I went in there was an officer in charge. That was my first meeting with Robert Barton. He was awfully nice. He had an office in the gymnasium building. He brought me along to the prison buildings—N. Block—and there I met Batt. The visitors were ranged up outside a barbed wire fence. The prisoners were in fours with a soldier at each side and we got so many minutes—I forget how many—to talk to the prisoners. He was in good form but looked a bit unkept, having slept on the floor for several nights. He was with Sean T. O'Kelly, Hugh O'Hare and Douglas French-Mullen whose arm was bandaged. He was the only one of the four who had a Volunteer tunic on. We had no time for anything except a few details of business. Back in the office Mr. Barton, who treated me very kindly, handed me a parcel with the prisoner's effects. The next time I saw Batt was by chance on the street when prisoners were being marched along the street. Mrs. O'Keeffe saw me and asked me to come along down, that these prisoners were being deported and perhaps Batt and Paddy would be among them; and so they were. The soldier who was near Batt was decent and allowed me to walk beside him and I was able to ask him some questions about business matters. He was away for four months, first in Wandsworth and then in Frongoch. I still have a small copy of an *Imitation Of Christ* given to Batt in Wandsworth by Gearoid O'Sullivan with the date of his release inscribed in it.

10.   There is not much of any importance that I remember during the remainder of the year. I know that my husband and the others of the Volunteers who were free were doing their best to keep the movement alive while the leaders were in prison.

11.   Tomás Ashe, of whom my husband always had a great opinion, came to stay with us for a week and he was coming back here after some meeting in the country where he expressed himself very strongly against the government, when he was arrested. He was walking along the street with Micheál Ó Foghludha on the Saturday when the detectives—Hoey and Smith—walked up beside him and said they would have to arrest him. It was during that week that he sang for us the song he had composed and set to music himself, *Let Me Carry Your Cross For Ireland, Lord*. He never sang it for anyone else; he said he never had an opportunity. His death was the greatest tragedy of all.

On the morning before his arrest he apologised for the trouble he was giving me. That day I stood on the doorstep and watched him go down the road till he got on the tram. I shall always remember him as I saw him then. He was a beautiful man with his tall noble figure and lovely wavy hair. I still have a letter that he wrote to me from Mountjoy a short time before his death.

12.   As time went on meetings began to be held again in our house. Harry Boland, Cathal Brugha, Mick Collins, Austin Stack and several others used to come, and I knew them all intimately. Mick Collins was the one of those four that I knew the least because he was always too engrossed in his important occupations to take part in small talk. But the women who worked for him and with him overlooked that characteristic in him and did not expect anything different from him because they knew how much he had on his mind.

13.   One morning when I had finished doing my door-brasses and was coming in I saw a small man coming up the path. He was slightly lame and had a green shade over one eye. He asked was Mr. O'Connor in and I said *"Yes, Cathal"*. He laughed and took the shade off his eye and said *"That is bad; I thought nobody could recognise me in this disguise"*. He had just come by the boat from England where he had spent several months. I called out my husband who failed to recognise him as he had put on the eyeshade again. I gave him a cup of coffee and he said he would go to bed for a couple of hours until his wife got his message and came to see him. When my husband went to Mrs. Brugha's house with the message, Mick Collins happened to be there as he occasionally spent a night there, if it was convenient. Mick called at our house shortly after and asked to see Cathal, but as Cathal had told me that he was to be disturbed by nobody until his wife came, I was very firm and refused to let him up to the bedroom. About 11.30 Mrs. Brugha came and Cathal, who had not slept, although he had lain down, got up and dressed to go out. It was their son Rory's birthday and they were going into town to buy a present for him.

14.   When Harry Boland came home from America, his first meeting with the leaders here was at my house in Brendan Rd. It was on a Friday and I had to provide lunch for 11 men. I went for the fish. I was told there was none, but a man in the shop—Jimmy Dunn, he is now dead—recognised me and gave me the fish. I cooked it and gave it to the men with tea and bread and butter. I had to do everything myself because I could not, for reasons of security, keep a maid in the house, or even a daily woman.

15.   Mick Collins slept at our house on only two or three occasions—it was

too dangerous a place for him. On one of those occasions Mick, Harry Boland and Batt sat in the kitchen talking and enjoying a pleasant evening; I think it was after a meeting. They were discussing the life they had seen in various places. Mick Collins was describing the life he led in London and Batt was giving his experiences in America. Harry Boland, who was very gay and lighthearted, said there was no place like Dublin. He asked me was there anything as enjoyable as getting on an outside car on a bank holiday with a few friends and driving to the strawberry beds or some such place, singing the good old Dublin songs like *Cockles And Mussels*. When at last they decided to go to bed, Harry and Mick slept in the return room in the one bed, with the window open at the bottom so that if there was a raid they could slip out easily. I did not dare to go to bed, as I was always uneasy when any of the leaders was sleeping in the house. In the course of the night I opened the door of the bedroom gently and saw the two men sleeping quietly. Mick had his arm resting on the little table by the bed, with his revolver lying beside it.

16. I knew Austin Stack very well. He stayed often at our house in Brendan Road and I got to like him very much. He was very gentle and kind. Afterwards when the unfortunate split came and many people became very bitter against their old friends, he never did. I did not meet him for a long time but when I did—on the street—he greeted me as affectionately and warmly as ever. Miss O'Rahilly also has always remained very friendly.

17. De Valera joined the Volunteers the same time as my husband and they drilled in the same company in Donnybrook and Batt had a very high opinion of him. I knew his wife, Sinead Ó Flannagain very well even before she married. She was a very pretty girl. She used to take part in the competitions that were held at the aeridheachta given by the Gaelic League and Batt often told me about the look of satisfaction he saw in de Valera's face on one of those occasions when she came in first in the girls' race. He was then interested in her but not engaged to her.

18. Sinead Mason—now Mrs. Derrig—was a very capable girl who worked for Mick Collins and some of the others. She never talked about what she was doing and there was no fear that she would betray any of their secrets.

19. At a later stage the leaders used to hold their meetings elsewhere than in my house and I don't seem to remember so much about those years as I do about the time before the Rising. When I have an opportunity I shall go over my papers and see if there is anything of importance that I could give or lend you to copy.

Index

Dixon, H. 58,70
DMP 85,103
Dolan, S. 70,79
Dolphin's Barn 31
Donnybrook 31,44,46,98-9,134,137
Dublin Brigade 44,71,77
Dublin Castle 43,45,92,110,114,127
Duggan, E. 37,127
Dunn, J. 36

Eglinton Rd. 75
Emmett, R. 77
Etchingham, S. 100,118

Famine 8
Farrell, Mr. 112
Feeney, B. 22
Fenians 7,9,36-7,46,48-9,72,77,123
Ferran, Dr. 112
Fianna Eireann 47
Fianna Fail 6,18
Figgis, D. 58
Fine Gael 18
Fitzalan, Ld. 127
Fitzgerald, D. 62
Fitzgerald, Ld. 77
Fitzgerald, Ld. E. 77
Fogarty, Dr. 87
Foley, M. 34,79
Foran, T. 58
Forde, Mr. 46
Forster, R. 22
Four Courts 63
Freedom Clubs 35
Freemasons 15
Free State 40,63
Free State Dail 5
French-Mullen, D. 135
Frongoch 41,69 etc,135

GAA 35
Gaelic League 33-6,133,137
Gallagher, F. 6
Galway Co. Council 116
Garvin, T. 23
General Election 85
George, D.L 11,19,120
George, King 38,41,120
German Plot 82
Germans 50-1

Germany 17,26
Gifford, Grace 55
Ginnell, L. 68
Glasnevin 46
Gleeson & O'Deas 44
Glenaulin 39
Glorious Revolution 21
Gold 87-8,131
Griffith, A. 34-5,39,41,45-6,77,81-2,85,128
Guiney, A.G. 51

Hales, S. 70
Harcourt St. 94,116
Hayes, Dr. R. 58,95
Healy, T. 39-40
Helga, The 127
Hibernians 79-80
Himmler, H. 17
Hobson, B. 36
Hoey, Detective 135
Home Rule 7
Home Rule Act 43,45
Horgan, D. 51
Houlihan, G. 41
Hue & Cry 86
Humphrey, Mrs. 107

Imitation Of Christ 69,135
Immaculate Conception 72
Invincibles 8
IRA 85
Iran 11
IRB 5,9,21-2,24-5,35,50,77,133
Irish Freedom 37-38
Irish Magazine 16
Irish Parliamentary Party 33,79
Irish Press 6-7,10,18
Irish Volunteers 46-7,69
Irish World 46

Jameson 112-3
Japan 26
Joyce, J. 19

Keating Branch 34,77,133
Kelly, T. 42,60
Kettle, L. 43
Kilkenny 79
Killiney 92
Kilmainham 37,53 etc, 58
Kimmage 71

O'Hare, Hugh 135
O'Hegarty, D. 34,133
O'Hegarty, S. 39-40,133
O'Hehir, H. 58
O'Higgins, K. 13,15,127,131
O'Keeffe, Mrs. P. 61,100,135
O'Keeffe, P. 34,60-4,73,81-2,93,135
O'Kelly, S.T. 6, 58,64,133,135
O'Mahony, J. 58-9,63,71,72,79
O'Malley, E. 5
O'Meara, J. 82
O'Muirthuile, S. 79
O'Neill, L. 58-9
O'Neill, M. 114
O'Rahilly, Miss 137
O'Rahilly, The 36,43,93
O'Rahillys, The 134
O'Reilly, J. 96,114,117-8,129
O'Reilly, M.W. 70
O'Sullivan, G. 34,39,60-2,64,69,114,117-8,133,135
O'Sullivan, M. 20

Orangemen 43,45
Orr, Major 61-2
Oxford University 10

Pearse, P. 37,47,55,82
Pembroke Council 90
Penal Laws 15
Plunkett, Count 48-9,77-8
Plunkett, J. 55,58-9
Poppy Day 14
Portland Prison 93
Power, C. 34,39
Pro-Cathedral 47
Providence, R.I. 32

Quinslisk 113

Reading Jail 64,70
Redmond, Detective 112-3
Redmond, J. 45-6
Reynolds, J.J. 59
RIC 85,105-6
Richmond Barracks 36,42,55,57etc,63-4,111,134
Richmond Rd. 37
Ringsend 30
Roscommon North 77
Rotunda Rink 43

Russia 26

Sallins 35
Sampson, W. 17
Sarsfield, P. 8,131
Sears, W. 64
Serbia 24
Sinn Fein 46
Sinn Fein 14,22-3,37,77,80,82,85,90,94,131
Sinn Fein Courts 90
Smuts, Gen. 120
Spike Island 30
Smith, Sgt. 36,135
Stack, A. 50,95,107,136-7
Staines, M. 44,71
Stephens, J. 37
Stephen's Green 93-4
Strafford, Ld. 14
Street, C.J.C. 22
Sullivan, J. 54,64

Taylor, Sir J. 92
Teeling Club 36
Thomas, J.H. 6-7
Thornton, F. 20
Tobin, L. 20,96,112,118-9
Tone, T.W. 35,41,77
Treaty 7,9-10,14-16,19,93,123 etc.
Treaty of Paris 10,13
Truce 13,93,98,100,120,126
Turkey 11-12

UCC 34
United Irishman 35
United Irishmen 17, 89

Vinegar Hill 44-5
Volunteers 43-4133,135,137

Walsh, J.J. 82
Walsh, P. 9,27
Wandsworth Jail 63,70,135
Wexford 8
White, Henry 26
White, T. de V. 13,16
Woods, Mrs. A. 100
World War I 8,14-6,20,23-4,26
World War II 11
Wormwood Scrubs 73-4

Young Ireland 21

Zimbabwe 24

AUBANE HISTORICAL SOCIETY

* **Ned Buckley's Poems**
* **St. John's Well**, by *Mary O'Brien*
* **Canon Sheehan: A Turbulent Priest**, by *B. Clifford*
* **A North Cork Anthology**, by *Jack Lane* and *B. Clifford*
* **Local Evidence to the Devon Commission**, by *Jack Lane*
* **Spotlights On Irish History**, by *Brendan Clifford*: Battles of Knocknanoss & Knockbrack, Edmund Burke, The Famine, The Civil War, John Philpot Curran, Daniel O'Connell and Roy Foster's approach to history.
* **The 'Cork Free Press' In The Context Of The Parnell Split: The Restructuring Of Ireland, 1890-1910,** by *Brendan Clifford*
* **Aubane: Where In The World Is It? A Microcosm Of Irish History In A Cork Townland,** by *Jack Lane*
* **Piarais Feiritéir: Dánta/Poems**, with *Translations* by *Pat Muldowney* **Audio tape** of a selection of the poems by *Bosco O'Conchuir*
* **Elizabeth Bowen: *"Notes On Eire"*.** Espionage Reports to Winston Churchill, 1940-42; With a Review of Irish Neutrality in WW II by *Jack Lane and Brendan Clifford*
* **The Life and Death of Mikie Dineen,** by *Jack Lane*
* **Aubane School and its Roll Books,** by *Jack Lane*
* **Kilmichael: the false surrender**. A discussion *by Peter Hart, Padraig O' Cuanacháin, D. R. O'Connor Lysaght, Dr Brian Murphy and Meda Ryan* with "Why the ballot was followed by the bullet", by *J. Lane & B.Clifford*.
* **Thomas Davis,** by *Charles Gavan Duffy*
* **Extracts from 'The Nation', 1842-44**.
* **Evidence to the Parnell Commission,** by *Jeremiah Hegarty, Canon Griffin and Dr Tanner MP*
* **Notes on the history of Millstreet,** by *Canon Michael Costello and Pádraig O'Maidín*
* **A Millstreet Medley,** by *various authors with rediscovered material by Canon Sheehan and Eoghan Ruadh O'Súilleabháin*
* **Millstreet—"the cockpit of Ireland",** by *various authors*
* **Aubane versus Oxford—a response to Professor Roy Foster and Bernard O'Donoghue,** by *various authors*
* **Millstreet—a "considerable town",** by *various authors*
* **A Millstreet Miscellany** *by various authors*
* **The 'Boys' of the Millstreet Battalion Area**—Some personal accounts of War of Independence, by *veterans of the Battalion*
* ***Na hAislingí*—vision poems of Eoghan Ruadh O'Súilleabháin** *translated by Pat Muldowney*, with Revisionist History of the 18th century under the Spotlight, by *Brendan Clifford*
* **D.D. Sheehan: Why He Left Cork In 1918**—A Correspondence from *The Corkman*.
* **The Burning Of Cork** (1920) by *Alan Ellis*, and other items.
* **Sean Moylan.** *In His Own Words.*